The most sublime mystery in the Christian faith is the incarnation of God in Christ. "The Word became flesh and blood, and moved into the neighborhood" (John 1:14), as Eugene Peterson's memorable translation puts it. Now Derek Vreeland has adapted *The Message* translation to lead us in a biblical exploration of this sublime mystery. *Incarnation* introduces the Advent Scripture texts in a fresh way for small groups and individuals alike.

BRIAN ZAHND, author of *The Wood Between the Worlds*

There's no idea more scandalous, more upending, more essential to understanding God and our own life than the incarnation. Vreeland artfully guides us into Scripture's wild country, where we see with fresh eyes the wonder of the human God.

WINN COLLIER, pastor, director of the Eugene Peterson Center for Christian Imagination, and author of *A Burning in My Bones: The Authorized Biography of Eugene H. Peterson* and *Love Big, Be Well*

No doctrine or creed is as dear to my soul as the doctrine of the incarnation. It is in God coming to us in the flesh, in Jesus Christ, that we can know "God's neighboring presence." In this fine book, Derek Vreeland walks us through Scripture to help us discover what all this means for our lives. As I read each page, answering the questions and reflecting, I grew deeper in knowing the God who meets us in our lives, and I hope you will too.

DAVID FITCH, Lindner Chair of Evangelical Theology at Northern Seminary and author of *Faithful Presence*

Incarnation is a rich, accessible, and Spirit-attuned resource that invites readers to see and celebrate the nearness of God in the real neighborhoods of our lives. With theological depth and pastoral warmth, Derek Vreeland leads us into Scripture using the down-to-earth beauty of *The Message* translation to reveal the wonder of God made flesh. What I love most about this study is how it keeps our eyes on Jesus—God with us—and at the same time helps us imagine how that truth reshapes how we live with and for our neighbors. This is not a sentimental Advent study. It is prophetic and hopeful, grounded and transformative. I wholeheartedly commend it to individuals and communities seeking to live out the incarnation with authenticity, justice, and joy.

JULIET LIU, pastor of Life on the Vine Christian Community

I can remember my neighbor coming to my door when I was a young boy. "Can you come out and play?" This book brought back memories of this invitation. This is not a study designed to help us think about the mystery of incarnation. This is an invitation to come and fully participate with the Christ. This isn't just about understanding the incarnation in a historical moment—it is about seeing the incarnation in our own lives today.

MARTY SOLOMON, author of *Asking Better Questions of the Bible* and creator of *The BEMA Podcast*

The mystery and beauty of the incarnation are truly worth exploring, and Derek Vreeland serves as a thoughtful guide in this excellent Bible study. I especially appreciate the way each lesson is structured in four sections, offering space for journaling and prayer. It's a rich resource—perfect for personal reflection as well as group study.

TIM WILDSMITH, pastor, professor, YouTuber, and author of *Bible Translations for Everyone* and *Daily Scripture Guidebook*

INCARNATION

GOD IN THE NEIGHBORHOOD BIBLE STUDIES

8 Lessons on How God Meets Us

DEREK VREELAND

Published in alliance with Tyndale House Publishers

NavPress.com

Incarnation: 8 Lessons on How God Meets Us

A NavPress resource published in alliance with Tyndale House Publishers

The Team:
David Zimmerman, Publisher; Olivia Eldredge, Acquisitions Editor; Elizabeth Schroll, Copyeditor; Lacie Phillips, Production Assistant; Eva M. Winters, Designer; Sarah Ocenasek, Proofreading Coordinator

For information about special discounts for bulk purchases, please contact Tyndale House Publishers at csresponse@tyndale.com, or call 1-855-277-9400.

ISBN 978-1-64158-984-0

Printed in the United States of America

31 30 29 28 27 26 25
7 6 5 4 3 2 1

To Wesley

May God bless and keep you always

CONTENTS

As We Begin:
An Introduction to Incarnation 1

LESSON 1 God Rules 7

LESSON 2 Playing War No More 19

LESSON 3 Looking for a Crop of Justice 33

LESSON 4 A Virgin Will Get Pregnant 47

LESSON 5 A Child Has Been Born for Us 59

LESSON 6 Messiah and Master 73

LESSON 7 The Word in the Neighborhood 85

LESSON 8 Unforced Rhythms of Grace 99

As We Go 111

Acknowledgments 113

Notes 115

The Word became flesh and blood,
    and moved into the neighborhood.
We saw the glory with our own eyes,
    the one-of-a-kind glory,
    like Father, like Son,
Generous inside and out,
    true from start to finish.

JOHN 1:14

AS WE BEGIN

An Introduction to Incarnation

I find it interesting that while he is the primary character of the story the Bible is telling, Jesus isn't named until we are three-quarters of the way through, when we turn the page from the Old Testament to the New Testament and read, "The family tree of Jesus Christ, David's son, Abraham's son" (Matthew 1:1). And yet Jesus is the central figure the Old Testament has been preparing us for. Speaking of the Old Testament law, Paul writes, "The earlier revelation was intended simply to get us ready for the Messiah" (Romans 10:4).

The Gospel writers, particularly John, announce that Jesus is the Word who "became flesh and blood, / and moved into the neighborhood" (John 1:14). The Word who has always been present to God, the Word who was *and is* God, is the one and only Son of God, sent by the Father to reveal the Father's heart for the world. Though John makes the bold declaration that no one at any time has ever seen God (John 1:18), John also proclaims remarkable news: The Word who moved into the neighborhood, "who exists at the very heart of the Father, / has made him plain as day" (John 1:18).

John's announcement comes in fulfillment of God's message given to Judah through the prophet Zechariah:

> "Shout and celebrate, Daughter of Zion!
> I'm on my way. I'm moving into your neighborhood!"
> God's Decree.

> Many godless nations will be linked up with God at that time. ("They will become my family! I'll live in their homes!")
>
> ZECHARIAH 2:1-10

God long ago promised to be with the ancient people of God. God promised a sign that exile would come to an end. The promise of God's presence wasn't only for ancient Judah and Israel but for many nations! All nations would be invited into God's family. Gentile nations didn't know the God of Israel, but Jesus has made God known to them—and to us. Like ancient Israel, we desire God's presence, for the Creator-God to live with us in our neighborhoods. When God is with us, we have the assurance that everything is going to be okay. When God is with us, we have peace in the present and hope for the future. But before Jesus came, we Gentiles didn't know who God was.

If we want to know what God is like, we look to Jesus, who is fully God, the full and definitive revelation of God. When Philip, one of the twelve apostles, asked Jesus to show them the Father, Jesus replied, "To see me is to see the Father" (John 14:9). Jesus gives God a face. Jesus shows us that the God of creation, the God of Abraham, Isaac, and Jacob, the God of the Hebrew prophets, is *for* us and *with* us. God saw the plight of the human condition, and God came to us. The Word moved into our neighborhood, and Jesus, the Word made flesh and blood, is here to stay.

The following eight lessons are organized around the themes of Advent and the incarnation, preparing for and celebrating the birth of Jesus and all it signifies. We begin in the Psalms, with Psalm 97, which celebrates God coming to meet us as King and planting "joy-seeds" in our hearts (Psalm 97:11).

The next four lessons lead us through key sections from the Old Testament, including Isaiah 2:1-5; Isaiah 5:1-23; and Isaiah 7:13-17; and culminating in Isaiah 9:1-7. These passages forecast the coming of Jesus, the Messiah, who will lead the nations to the mountain of God and establish peace and justice. Importantly, they describe Jesus as the son born of a virgin, the one coming to "rule from the historic David throne" (Isaiah 9:7).

Lesson 6 leads us into the New Testament, to the account of the birth of Jesus in Luke 2. Lesson 7 explores the beginning of John's Gospel, where we encounter the Word, who "became flesh and blood, / and moved into the neighborhood" (John 1:14). We conclude in Matthew's Gospel with Jesus, who is God-With-Us, teaching us how to live "freely and lightly" in God's "unforced rhythms of grace" (Matthew 11:29-30). Lesson by lesson we are drawn into the story of God, humanity's undoing of God's good world through sin, and God's desire to come to us in order to rescue us.

This Bible study series uses the beauty and sacredness of ordinary language found in *The Message*, a contemporary and imaginative translation of the Bible, to lead you on a journey through the Scriptures to encounter Jesus in his life, death, and resurrection. The series is broken into three parts:

Book 1, *Incarnation*, dives deep into the mystery of the incarnation, where God meets us, joining us in life.

Book 2, *Crucifixion*, reflects on Jesus' execution, where God joins us in death, and in doing so, saves us.

Book 3, *Resurrection*, leads us on an Easter journey, where God joins us in life anew to restore us to what we were created to be: image bearers of the God of love.

When we realize that God is with us in life, we *come alive*. When we understand that God is with us in death, we *believe*. When we experience God-With-Us in new life, we *participate*. These studies are designed to bring you into "God's neighboring presence," a phrase I picked up from Eugene Peterson.[1] The coming of Jesus marks God moving into our neighborhood, and he is present with us as personally as any of our neighbors.

How to Use This Bible Study

Lessons in these Bible studies are designed for either individual reflection or group study in small groups, Sunday school classes, or home groups. You are invited to use these Bible studies for your own personal growth and spiritual formation. Lessons are made up of four parts—"The Approach," "The Word," "The Neighborhood," and "The Prayer." Here is how each lesson is structured.

The Approach: Setting the Scene

We begin with an introduction to the Scripture passage from *The Message* we will cover in each lesson. "The Approach" ends with starter questions to get you thinking (if you are reading on your own) or to help your group begin sharing with one another.

The Word: Diving into Scripture

Following our introduction and opening questions, we turn our attention to a particular passage of Scripture and dig in, looking at the uniqueness of the language of *The Message*. In his translation, Eugene Peterson sought to break down the dividing wall between so-called secular and so-called sacred language. For Peterson, *all* language is sacred because it is all a gift from God.[2] Questions are provided here, as well, to encourage you to enter the text more fully.

The Neighborhood: Living It Out

We will wrap up each lesson by looking outward toward our own neighborhoods, asking how the passage of Scripture calls us to live in the way of Jesus while we are among our real flesh-and-blood neighbors. Following Jesus is not merely gaining knowledge and categorizing God facts. Following Jesus is a way of living shaped by the Holy Spirit around the death and resurrection of Jesus so that our lives look like dying to self and rising to reflect the life of Jesus. Reflection questions guide this outward focus on how we live in our neighborhoods filled with real people who may or may not identify as Christians.

The Prayer: Drawing Near to God

Each lesson concludes with a prayer drawn from the specific Bible passage used in that lesson.

There are companion videos available on my website here:

Before You Start

If you are using these Bible studies on your own, find a quiet and comfortable place to read. Before you start a lesson, take a deep breath, exhale slowly, and offer a brief prayer. Ask the Holy Spirit to work with Holy Scripture to show you the ways of Jesus. As you are reading, feel free to jot down responses to the questions throughout each lesson.

If you are using these Bible studies in a group, take turns introducing yourself to the group; perhaps you could each share why you are in this Bible study or what you hope to get out of it. Open with prayer, asking Jesus to pour out the Holy Spirit on your group so that the Holy Spirit will be your teacher and guide. Identify a group leader to guide the conversation. Give people a few moments to reflect on the questions through the study, and then invite them to share with the group their thoughts and answers to the questions. Don't rush people to answer. Trust and learn from silence.

Whether you're doing this study on your own or in community, if you are able, read all Scripture passages out loud and pray the prayer at the end of each lesson aloud.

I love Jesus. I've loved Jesus since I was fifteen years old, and after all these years, I *still* love Jesus, because he never ceases to amaze and surprise me. And I love leading Bible studies, because when we take time to study Holy Scripture, God always surprises me with new details that make me ponder. My prayer is that you will grow in gratitude through these Bible studies and see with greater clarity what God has done for us in and through Jesus. I pray you will grow in your knowledge of the ways of Jesus and feel the nudging of the Holy Spirit to live out what you believe.

Derek Vreeland
Advent 2024

LESSON 1

GOD RULES

The Approach

I have come to see that we live in a God-saturated world.

All creation participates in the life of God. This participation includes human beings—regular people like you and me—who bear God's image. We all live our day-to-day lives surrounded by God's presence, whether we are aware of it or not. And to be honest, many of us are not aware.

It's not as if God pops into our world now and again, does something amazing, and then leaves. Rather, God is always here, blanketing us with an unseen presence. God isn't hiding out in suburban churches, back-alley chapels, and ancient cathedrals (though God can certainly be found in those places). The Creator-God, who has been revealed in Jesus and by the Holy Spirit, is present everywhere, meaning God is knowable, findable, and contactable. Even in our loneliest moments of isolation, God is there. We are all participating, with everything else God has made, in the presence of God.

Preaching at the Areopagus in Athens, the apostle Paul proclaimed about God,

> "Starting from scratch, he made the entire human race and made the earth hospitable, with plenty of time and space for living so we could seek after God, and not just grope around in the dark but actually *find* him. He doesn't play hide-and-seek with us. He's not remote; he's *near*. We live and move in him, can't get away from him! One of your poets said it well: 'We're the God-created.' Well, if we are the God-created, it doesn't make a lot of sense to think we could hire a sculptor to chisel a god out of stone for *us*, does it?"
>
> ACTS 17:26-29

We live in the world God made.

We move about our days in a world filled with the presence of God.

We can't quite find a place where we cannot encounter God. King David poetically poses the questions "Is there anyplace I can go to avoid your Spirit? / to be out of your sight? / If I climb to the sky, you're there! / If I go underground, you're there!" (Psalm 139:7-8). The Creator-God can be accessed from all places in creation, even desecrated ones.

While followers of Jesus have always worshiped God and participated in the life of God, you and I have been born into a world structured in such a way that we forget that God is near. We live in a secular age where the signposts and reminders of God's presence continue to diminish. Remnants of the God made famous by Jesus linger on in fragments in our culture, but they end up being collected and stowed away as relics of a bygone age. Images of God have been shifted to the periphery of society. Slowly and subtly, the God who created us for connectivity seems more and more out of reach.

Jesus moved into the neighborhood not only so we could see what God is like but also to reveal that the God of creation is *with us* and *for us*. We can find the root of this God-given revelation in the worship of the ancient people of God recorded in the Psalms. This collection of psalms is the original hymnal and prayer book of the church, and it provides us with the basic vocabulary for Christian prayer. The book also helps us get a sense of the story of ancient Israel with the themes of creation, covenant, worship, monarchy, and justice.

The entire collection of psalms resounds with praise for God, the King of Israel. The presence of God among God's people was—and is—a ruling and guiding presence: God is among us as *King*. The ancient people of God had the audacity to proclaim through their worship that their God, the God of Israel, was not only King of Israel but also King of the world! Throughout the Psalms, the God of Israel is celebrated as the King who is near.

Before we look at a particular psalm, take a moment to reflect on these questions.

1. Where did you grow up? How did that region influence how you understand life? God? Family? Relationships?

2. Where do you most often experience God's presence? In the beauty of creation? In worship with your church? Alone in prayer? During some other activity?

3. What signposts in our culture still point people to the reality of God's presence with us?

The Word

Imagine Jewish families traveling to Jerusalem for one of their many festivals, chanting and singing songs praising the absolute sovereignty of their God over all the gods of their pagan neighbors. Every tribe surrounding ancient Israel had their gods who ruled over their territory. But the children of Abraham had the unbashful boldness—the chutzpah—to declare that *their* God was the one true King ruling all of it. They believed that God, as Creator of all the peoples of the earth, ruled as King and Lord over all:

> Sing songs to God, sing out!
>   Sing to our King, sing praise!
> He's *Lord over earth*,
>   so sing your best songs to God.
> God is Lord of godless nations—
>   sovereign, he's King of the mountain.
>
> PSALM 47:6-8 (EMPHASIS ADDED)

The idea of God as King is essential to understanding why the coming of Jesus as the Word is such good news. God comes to be with us in Jesus, who through his sacrificial death and subsequent resurrection is the King of all kings and Lord of all lords. We see the theme of the kingly nature of God repeatedly in the Psalms:

GOD is King, robed and ruling,
 GOD is robed and surging with strength.
PSALM 93:1

GOD is the best,
 High King over all the gods.
PSALM 95:3

Fill the air with praises to King GOD.
PSALM 98:6

GOD has set his throne in heaven;
 he rules over us all. He's the King!
PSALM 103:19

Psalm 97 opens in similar fashion—proclaiming that God rules. I love this psalm because it echoes the language of God as King, an important theme of the gospel. Theologian and author Matthew Bates addresses why we need the gospel. The answer he gives is simple: "We need a king."[1] And like many of the psalms, Psalm 97 is packed with imagery that enlivens our imaginations for seeing God's neighboring presence with us.

Let's look at this psalm one section at a time.

GOD rules: *there's* something to shout over!
On the double, mainlands and islands—celebrate!
PSALM 97:1

While some modern English translations, like the NRSV and NLT, open with "The Lord is king," *The Message* begins Psalm 97 in a more traditional, although slightly nuanced, way: "God rules." As an opening statement of worship, "God rules" evokes the dynamic and active nature of God's Kingdom. The God who rules and reigns is the Lord, Yahweh, the God of Israel. He does indeed reign as King.

> Bright clouds and storm clouds circle 'round him;
> Right and justice anchor his rule.
>
> PSALM 97:2

How does God rule? What values mark God's administration? God's rule is anchored by "right and justice." The image of an anchor, like that of a foundation, implies the steady, unmoving nature of God's Kingdom. While human leaders rule by popular opinion or hubris, God rules according to righteousness and justice. The *rightness* and *justness* of God are not on the periphery of the Kingdom of God; they anchor it.

> Fire blazes out before him,
> Flaming high up the craggy mountains.
>
> His lightnings light up the world;
> Earth, wide-eyed, trembles in fear.
>
> The mountains take one look at God
> And melt, melt like wax before earth's Lord.
>
> PSALM 97:3-5

In the ancient world, and in the world today, fire dazzles the imagination. The metaphorical flames dancing around God's throne rise "high up the craggy mountains" that surround God in an intimidating posture, but these are the same mountains that "melt like wax" before the Lord. Mountains adversarial to the Kingdom of God can seem insurmountable to humans, but God is King of the whole earth, and ultimately, they are defeated by the fire of God's roaring love.

> The heavens announce that he'll set everything right,
> And everyone will see it happen—glorious!
>
> PSALM 97:6

And now we hear the heavens speaking, making an announcement as the mountains melt. The heavens announce the righteousness of God, which *The Message* translates here as God's work to "set everything right." God has moved into our neighborhood to set right a neighborhood gone wrong. In this psalm, the righteousness implied is not God's own moral rightness but God's desire to set right that which has gone wrong.

> All who serve handcrafted gods will be sorry—
> And they were so proud of their ragamuffin gods!
>
> On your knees, all you gods—worship him!
> And Zion, you listen and take heart!
>
> Daughters of Zion, sing your hearts out:
> God has done it all, has set everything right.
>
> PSALM 97:7-8

Everything we worship in place of God is an idol, a "handcrafted god," an image of the divine we cobble together from our own desires and tastes. These shabby "ragamuffin gods" never offer us the life we were created to live, yet we continue to esteem them. Judgment lies in wait when we worship these handcrafted gods. But the good—and somewhat unexpected—news is that God's judgment is not merely punitive but restorative. In God's judgment, God seeks to be *with us* to make things right with us and the world.

> You, God, are High God of the cosmos,
> Far, far higher than any of the gods.
>
> God loves all who hate evil,
> And those who love him he keeps safe,
> Snatches them from the grip of the wicked.
>
> PSALM 97:9-10

God is simultaneously *transcendent* and *immanent*, something we only find in the God made famous by Jesus. God is both high and lifted up and intimately connected to the world God loves.

Praise is the proper response to God's acts of *rightness* and *justness* in the world. God bends his love toward those who cast down their idols and cast off the evil associated with those fake gods. Through our acts of worship and repentance, we experience the presence of Emmanuel ("God-With-Us") to rescue us and keep us safe.

> Light-seeds are planted in the souls of God's people,
> Joy-seeds are planted in good heart-soil.
>
> So, God's people, shout praise to God,
> Give thanks to our Holy God!
>
> PSALM 97:11-12

Most English translations open verse 11 with the mildly prosaic line "Light is sown for the righteous" (Psalm 97:11, ESV). *The Message* greets us with "Light-seeds are planted in the souls of God's people." As the people of God, we are the righteous, and the light that emanates from God's rule and reign gets planted in our hearts, that it might bear the fruit of righteousness and justice. For that, we give God thanks.

Take some time to reflect on these questions.

4. When you hear the word *king*, what is the first thought or image that comes to mind?

5. What are the differences between interpreting God's righteousness as God's moral purity and interpreting it as God's desire to set things right?

6. An idol is any person, idea, thing, pursuit, or agenda we put in the place of God. What are some popular "handcrafted" and "ragamuffin" gods you see people worshiping in your neighborhood and community?

7. In what ways do the false gods worshiped as idols cause damage in our world?

8. What "light-seeds" has the Holy Spirit planted in your heart?

The Neighborhood

Jesus comes as the Word of God moving into our neighborhood to rule, but he doesn't rule like other earthly kings. He comes to rule with healing in his hands and the message of mercy on his lips. He doesn't come to take over so much as to *make over* this world God loves. Our response to God's work in our neighborhood is participation through acts of worship and justice.

9. How does the kingly presence of God-With-Us inspire you to worship?

10. What would it look like if you became a light for God's love and practiced justice in your neighborhood?

The Prayer

As you continue to reflect on Psalm 97, offer this prayer.

God and Ruler over all, we submit ourselves to your rule. May you be high and exalted in our prayers and known through our acts of kindness and mercy. By your Spirit, enable us to perceive your work among us, and condition our hearts to be ready to serve. Lead us in the way of life everlasting, far away from the "ragamuffin gods" who tempt us to depart from your way. Come, Lord Jesus. We humbly pray this in your name. Amen.

LESSON 2

PLAYING WAR NO MORE

The Approach

I hate waiting.

At least in my natural state, setting aside all the work of grace in my life, I'm not a patient person. I thrive in the presence of speed and efficiency. As I compare my tendencies to the person and work of Jesus, I recognize my lack of patience as a deficiency. A rushed and impatient life is nothing to celebrate. A rushed decision is normally a wrong one. Folly follows right behind impatience. Fighting is often an act of impatience. Fighting—whether on the geopolitical scene or between neighbors in an apartment complex—often erupts because of our impatience, among other things. I certainly have not been the best version of myself when I've been restless and hurried. One gift Advent has given me has been the grace to grow in patience.

I didn't grow up paying much attention to the Christian calendar (also called the church year), with its liturgical seasons, like Advent, Lent, and Eastertide. The local church that nurtured me in the faith as a teenager taught me to love the Bible, but the words *Advent* and *Lent* aren't found there. I would later discover that Advent comes not from Scripture but from having been handed down to us by the great Christian tradition.

All local churches have traditions, even those who value a contemporary approach to their worship services. While not on the same level of authority as Scripture, tradition is respected; it's considered the collected wisdom of the past. As author G. K. Chesterton writes in his much-celebrated book *Orthodoxy*, "Tradition means giving votes to the most obscure of all classes, our ancestors. It is the democracy of the dead. Tradition refuses to submit to the small and arrogant oligarchy of those who merely happen to be walking about."[1]

Appreciating the great Christian tradition has played a major role in my own spiritual formation. As I continue to walk with Jesus and seek to become more like him, I have found value in observing the seasons on this sacred calendar because the Christian calendar tells the story of Jesus. This calendar begins with the season of Advent, which is marked by the four Sundays before Christmas Day. During Advent, we slow down the busyness of the holiday season, and we wait, allowing the anticipation of celebrating Jesus' birth to grow in our hearts. Advent resists war's impetuous lack of patience and teaches us to wait.

During the Christmas season (traditionally called Christmastide), we celebrate the incarnation, that is, Immanuel, God-With-Us, the Word moving into the neighborhood. Since we hold the celebration of the birth of Jesus in such high esteem, we take four weeks to prepare for its arrival. During Advent, we remind ourselves once again why God came to join us. We remind ourselves of the brokenness in the world and our need for

- a Savior to rescue us,
- a Deliverer to upend injustice,
- a Healer to mend what is broken, and
- a Shepherd to lead us to that place of life everlasting.

Advent gives us hope that the God who "bans war from pole to pole" and "breaks all the weapons across his knee" (Psalm 46:9) is coming to rescue us. Advent counteracts the shallow sentimentality that reduces Christmas to cheap entertainment and a cultural commodity. It reminds us that not all is well with God's good world. So we slow down during the four weeks of Advent. While it's true that Christmas joy slips into the Advent season, there is wisdom in not jumping too quickly to Christmas. Formation happens in the waiting.

The prophet Isaiah stands out as a great guide for Advent. After all, many of the Christmas prophecies we treasure are found in Isaiah. His prophecies come to us with poetic language that stirs our imagination. Concerning this prophet, Eugene Peterson writes,

> For Isaiah, words are watercolors and melodies and chisels to make truth and beauty and goodness. Or, as the case may be, hammers and swords and scalpels to unmake sin and guilt and rebellion. Isaiah does not merely convey information. He creates visions, delivers revelation, and arouses belief. He is a poet in the most fundamental sense—a maker, making God present and that presence urgent. Isaiah is the supreme poet-prophet to come out of the Hebrew people.[2]

Before we look at what Isaiah has to say in his melodic, watercolor prophecies, take a moment to reflect on these questions.

1. What traditions did you grow up with in your home or at church during Christmastime?

2. Do you consider yourself a naturally patient person? Why or why not?

3. Why is it important to consider Isaiah a poet? What can we expect from his prophecies?

The Word

As a poet-prophet, Isaiah provides, in the words of Old Testament scholar Walter Brueggemann, a "prophetic imagination" by both criticizing and energizing Israel.[3] Isaiah opens his book of prophecies speaking on God's behalf to ancient Jerusalem before the Babylonian exile. He criticizes them for their "worship charades" (Isaiah 1:13) and injustice, which culminated in Judah (the southern kingdom of the divided monarchy) walking out on their God. Isaiah writes,

Heaven and earth, you're the jury.
 Listen to God's case:
"I had children and raised them well,
 and they turned on me.
The ox knows who's boss,
 the mule knows the hand that feeds him,
But not Israel.
 My people don't know up from down.
Shame! Misguided God-dropouts,
 staggering under their guilt-baggage,
Villainous gang,
 band of vandals—
My people have walked out on me, their God,
 turned their backs on The Holy of Israel,
walked off and never looked back."

ISAIAH 1:2-4

Isaiah follows his jarring words of criticism with energizing words of hope:

"Come. Sit down. Let's argue this out."
 This is God's Message:

> "If your sins are blood-red,
>   they'll be snow-white.
> If they're red like crimson,
>   they'll be like wool.
> If you'll willingly obey,
>   you'll feast like kings.
> But if you're willful and stubborn,
>   you'll die like dogs."
> That's right. GOD says so.
>
> ISAIAH 1:18-20

God offered hope to Judah, just as God offers us hope today. Sins can be forgiven. The people of Judah then, like us now, could return to God and walk in the way of loving obedience and feast like kings! The alternative was bleak—remain in a state of stubbornness and die like dogs. Ouch! Isaiah's prophetic criticism cuts like a knife.

Isaiah's hope surges in chapter 2. Isaiah paints his prophetic hope using the metaphor of a mountain, a common image for the people of God. Think of Mount Sinai, where God gave the law to Moses, or Mount Carmel, where Elijah held his showdown with the prophets of Baal. Or consider the Mount of Transfiguration, where Moses and Elijah mystically met with Jesus in his divine glory and heard God the Father speaking. Throughout Scripture we encounter mountains as sacred places. They serve as emblems of God's desire to be present with God's people.[4] The mountain Isaiah describes is not just for Judah but for all nations! Let's take a look at that mountain:

> The Message Isaiah got regarding Judah and Jerusalem:
>
> There's a day coming
>   when the mountain of GOD's House
> Will be The Mountain—
>   solid, towering over all mountains.

> All nations will river toward it,
>   people from all over set out for it.
>
> ISAIAH 2:1-2

God has always wanted to be a Father with a big, multiethnic family. The Bible shows this clearly from the call of Abraham in Genesis 12. God didn't choose the ancient Hebrews because God only wanted one ethnic people in God's family. Instead, God chose Abram (whose name was later changed to Abraham) so that through his descendants God could bless all families of the earth. This is how Jewish election works: The Hebrews were elected to be the chosen people not so God would save one group of people and discard the rest. Rather, God chose them so that *through* them God could open the road to the mountain of God's house for *all* people. Even as Judah faced the imminent threat of exile in a foreign nation, Isaiah offered hope that one day all nations would set a course for God's mountain home:

> They'll say, "Come,
>   let's climb GOD's Mountain,
>   go to the House of the God of Jacob.
> He'll show us the way he works
>   so we can live the way we're made."
> Zion's the source of the revelation.
>   GOD's Message comes from Jerusalem.
>
> ISAIAH 2:3

What a thrilling image! Not only will God open the road to all nations to come to the mountain of God, but the nations will also put forth the effort to climb that mountain, to draw near the God of Abraham, Isaac, and Jacob, the one true God of creation. They will come to learn the ways of God—the way God works in the world—so that they can say, "We can live the way we're made." Most English translations accurately render this verse "There he will teach us his ways, and we will *walk in his paths*" (Isaiah 2:3, NLT; emphasis added). Yet *The Message* goes deeper, capturing the heart of what it means to walk in God's paths. In walking God's way, we can live the way we were made to as image bearers of God. We were created by the God who is love to walk in the ways of love. When we walk on another path, we are not being true to who God made us to be.

> He'll settle things fairly between nations.
> He'll make things right between many peoples.
> They'll turn their swords into shovels,
> their spears into hoes.
> No more will nation fight nation;
> they won't play war anymore.
>
> ISAIAH 2:4

How is God going to have all ethnic groups and nationalities live together on God's mountain? He's going to teach them to play war no more. God will settle their disputes in a fair manner and teach them how to turn weapons for fighting into implements of farming. We cannot accomplish this peaceful coexistence on our own, not with the current state of our divided neighborhoods and fractured world. We need God to come in human flesh and show us how to live without fighting. We need God to move into our neighborhood and demonstrate the way of forgiveness and compassion and, most of all, peace. *Do you have the capacity to hope for a world without war—a world without global wars and a world without interpersonal wars?* Let hope grow that one day people will be playing war no more.

> Come, family of Jacob,
> let's live in the light of GOD.
>
> ISAIAH 2:5

God's light of hope shone so brightly that Isaiah called Judah to begin to live in that light in the present moment. God's light is beautiful to behold. In the light of God, we see all things as they truly are. Yet I find it difficult to imagine that the kingdom of Judah, which had been established by the warfare of King David, would have any way of knowing how to walk in God's light apart from fighting their enemies. Could they repent of their idolatry and injustice?

The story of Israel and Judah is a cyclical story of faithfulness, temptation, sin, judgment, repentance, and then faithfulness again. This story is repeated again and again in the Old Testament. Jesus brings the long-awaited conclusion to that story when he comes proclaiming, "I am the world's Light. No one who follows me stumbles around in the darkness. I provide plenty of light to live in" (John 8:12). Jesus is the Light of God in human flesh.

Take some time to reflect on these questions.

4. What images stand out to you from Isaiah's words in Isaiah 2:1-5?

5. In addition to Mount Sinai, Mount Carmel, and the Mount of Transfiguration, what other mountains do we see in the Bible? What do they represent?

6. What does it mean for us to "live the way we're made"?

7. Do you have any hope for peace to be present in our world today? When do you expect the kind of peace Isaiah describes here? When Jesus returns? In our world today? Perhaps then *and* now?

8. Think about the light of God's hope. What do you find beautiful? Helpful? What else do you feel about it?

The Neighborhood

As we cultivate this hope for peace, we are invited to live in that hope now. God has, after all, moved into our neighborhood. Jesus has come, teaching us to love our enemies and pray for those who persecute us. Jesus has shown us the way of loving God and loving our neighbors. Though not every person is steering the boat down the river toward the mountain of God, we are there now! We can begin to learn the ways of peace and forgiveness today in how we live in our neighborhoods so that we can reflect the light of God's love radiating from the face of Jesus.

9. What are some tangible things you can do to reject fighting and instead walk in God's light in your neighborhood?

10. Who do you need to pray for, offer forgiveness to, or seek reconciliation with? Make a plan for pursuing forgiveness and/or reconciliation.

The Prayer

Forgiveness and the work of reconciliation require emotional energy and spiritual strength. With forgiveness in mind, offer this prayer.

Lord Jesus, you taught us to pray with the words "Forgive us our trespasses, as we forgive those who have trespassed against us." Have mercy on us and help us as we live in the light of your love upon your holy mountain as a peace-loving people. Help us forgive and walk in forgiveness. Help us love the things that make for peace and live fully alive in your peaceable Kingdom. We humbly pray this in your name. Amen.

LESSON 3

LOOKING FOR A CROP OF JUSTICE

The Approach

I have finally come to recognize that *justice* is a Bible word.

It seems like a growing number of Christians get uneasy whenever the topic of justice is raised in the public square or from the pulpit. Sadly, people who love Jesus and have devoted themselves to reading and studying our sacred Scriptures assume that the term *justice* is only associated with social movements or, worse yet, political agendas. The truth is that the language—and practice—of justice doesn't belong to a specific social movement or certain political party. It belongs to the people of God!

A quick survey of how biblical writers use the word *justice* can reveal just how embedded the concept is within Christian faith and practice. As we saw in lesson 1, the very throne of God is anchored in justice: "Bright clouds and storm clouds circle 'round him; / Right and justice anchor his rule" (Psalm 97:2). The collected wisdom of Proverbs associates justice with the righteous: "Good people celebrate when justice triumphs, / but for the workers of evil it's a bad day" (Proverbs 21:15). And the Law and the Prophets resound with the theme of justice:

God's curse on anyone who interferes with justice due the foreigner, orphan, or widow.
All respond: *Yes. Absolutely.*

DEUTERONOMY 27:19

What are you waiting for? Return to your God!
Commit yourself in love, in justice!
Wait for your God,
and don't give up on him—ever!

HOSEA 12:6

[God said,] "I can't stand your religious meetings.
I'm fed up with your conferences and conventions.
I want nothing to do with your religion projects,
your pretentious slogans and goals. . . .
Do you know what I want?
I want justice—oceans of it.
I want fairness—rivers of it.
That's what I want. That's *all* I want."

AMOS 5:21-24

But me—I'm filled with God's power,
filled with God's Spirit of justice and strength,
Ready to confront Jacob's crime
and Israel's sin.

MICAH 3:8

Justice is God's work in setting things right. God's justice is God's *just-ness*, God's desire for what is fair and equitable. In the face of injustice in our world, we wait with anticipation for justice to come in the power of God's Kingdom. Jesus, God in human flesh, came to us proclaiming justice to all nations. Matthew notes that this proclamation fulfilled what Isaiah says about the coming Messiah:

Jesus, knowing they were out to get him, moved on. A lot of people followed him, and he healed them all. He also cautioned them to keep it quiet, following guidelines set down by Isaiah:

> Look well at my handpicked servant;
> I love him so much, take such delight in him.
> I've placed my Spirit on him;
> *he'll decree justice to the nations.*
> But he won't yell, won't raise his voice;
> there'll be no commotion in the streets.
> He won't walk over anyone's feelings,
> won't push you into a corner.
> Before you know it, *his justice will triumph*;
> the mere sound of his name will signal hope, even
> among far-off unbelievers.

MATTHEW 12:18-21 (EMPHASIS ADDED)

Matthew was quoting Isaiah 42:

> [The Lord said,] "Take a good look at my servant.
> I'm backing him to the hilt.
> He's the one I chose,
> and I couldn't be more pleased with him.
> I've bathed him with my Spirit, my *life*.
> *He'll set everything right among the nations.*
> He won't call attention to what he does
> with loud speeches or gaudy parades.
> He won't brush aside the bruised and the hurt
> and he won't disregard the small and insignificant,
> but he'll steadily and firmly set things right.

> He won't tire out and quit. He won't be stopped
> until he's finished his work—*to set things right on earth.*
> Far-flung ocean islands
> wait expectantly for his teaching."
>
> ISAIAH 42:1-4 (EMPHASIS ADDED)

The Message uses the phrases *set everything right* and *set things right* in this passage from Isaiah. This translation captures the essence of the Hebrew word *mishpat*, often translated "justice" in the Old Testament when related to God's activity. From a biblical point of view, justice isn't merely about punishment (although it may include it); biblical justice is more restorative than punitive. God desires to restore his image-bearing creatures to reflect God's image rightly in the world. God wants to set right a world gone wrong. The Bible's word for this is *justice*.

Take a moment to reflect on the following questions.

1. Proverbs 21:15 says, "Good people celebrate when justice triumphs." How do you celebrate when good things happen in your life?

2. If you could snap your fingers and cause one wrong thing in our world to be made right, what would it be?

3. Has your understanding of justice changed over the years? How would you describe the biblical concept of justice in your own words?

The Word

Matthew cites Isaiah in describing the work of Jesus because he wants to show the connection between the Old Testament Prophets and the ministry of Jesus. We'll inevitably misunderstand who Jesus is and what Jesus came to do without a thorough understanding of the Old Testament, which isn't a rule book for us to follow but rather the Spirit-inspired backstory to God's full revelation in Jesus Christ.

The theme of justice can be found throughout the Scriptures. Isaiah weaves the theme of justice throughout his poetic prophecies as recorded in the Old Testament. In the New Testament, Jesus emphasizes the importance of justice in his critique of the hypocrisy of the Pharisees: "What sorrow awaits you teachers of religious law and you Pharisees. Hypocrites! For you are careful to tithe even the tiniest income from your herb gardens, but you ignore the more important aspects of the law—justice, mercy, and faith. You should tithe, yes, but do not neglect the more important things" (Matthew 23:23-24, NLT). Justice is not tangential to the mission of Jesus; it is among the most important things in God's law of love, because God "loves righteousness and justice" (Psalm 33:5, ESV).

In Isaiah 5, the prophet communicates God's disgust with Israel and Judah for not pursuing justice. Later, Jesus would come as the Word of God to sum up Israel and Judah's entire purpose: to be God's peculiar people of worship and justice. But before we encounter the miracle of the Word moving into our world, we need to step back and see the backstory. Isaiah 5 offers us a poem, a ballad sung by the Lord. Isaiah's poem is set in a vineyard, an image that Jesus would later draw on in his teachings (see Matthew 21:33-41). Let's walk through this poem.

> I'll sing a ballad to the one I love,
>   a love ballad about his vineyard:
> The one I love had a vineyard,
>   a fine, well-placed vineyard.
> He hoed the soil and pulled the weeds,
>   and planted the very best vines.

He built a lookout, built a winepress,
    a vineyard to be proud of.
He looked for a vintage yield of grapes,
    but for all his pains he got garbage grapes.

"Now listen to what I'm telling you,
    you who live in Jerusalem and Judah.
What do you think is going on
    between me and my vineyard?
Can you think of anything I could have done
    to my vineyard that I didn't do?
When I expected good grapes,
    why did I get bitter grapes?"

ISAIAH 5:1-4

Pay attention to the images Isaiah describes—a vineyard, soil, weeds, vines, and grapes. In addition to the visual imagery presented in this poem, pay attention to the emotions being expressed as well. The Lord is singing this to Israel and Judah, who God loves. *What are the emotions behind these words?*

"Well now, let me tell you
    what I'll do to my vineyard:
I'll tear down its fence
    and let it go to ruin.
I'll knock down the gate
    and let it be trampled.
I'll turn it into a patch of weeds, untended, uncared for—
    thistles and thorns will take over.
I'll give orders to the clouds:
    'Don't rain on that vineyard, ever!'"

Do you get it? The vineyard of GOD-of-the-Angel-Armies
is the country of Israel.
All the men and women of Judah
are the garden he was so proud of.
He looked for a crop of justice
and saw them murdering each other.
He looked for a harvest of righteousness
and heard only the moans of victims.

ISAIAH 5:5-7

The emotions captured in verses 1-4 spill over into specific actions God promises to carry out, and the curtain is lifted on this poem: It's revealed that the vineyard represents Israel and Judah.

In addition to this metaphor, there is an intentional play on words in the last four lines that is hard to see in English: The Lord looked for a crop of justice (Hebrew: *mishpat*) and what God saw was them murdering each other (Hebrew: *mispach*). He looked for righteousness (Hebrew: *tzedaqah*) and heard only the moans of victims (Hebrew: *tzeaqah*). The Lord looked for good grapes, but all he got were "garbage grapes." And as a result, the Lord is dropping a series of dooms!

Doom to those who get up early
and start drinking booze before breakfast,
Who stay up all hours of the night
drinking themselves into a stupor.
They make sure their banquets are well-furnished
with harps and flutes and plenty of wine,
But they'll have nothing to do with the work of GOD,
pay no mind to what he is doing.

ISAIAH 5:11-12

Israel and Judah have succumbed to idolatry. They have ignored their God, and in place of working with God, they are partying with their friends. They have traded worship of the God of creation for worship of pleasure. Their desire for drunkenness has become their god. Idolatry has now led to injustice and more doom.

Doom to you who use lies to sell evil,
who haul sin to market by the truckload,
Who say, "What's God waiting for?
Let him get a move on so we can see it.
Whatever The Holy of Israel has cooked up,
we'd like to check it out."

Doom to you who call evil good
and good evil,
Who put darkness in place of light
and light in place of darkness,
Who substitute bitter for sweet
and sweet for bitter!

Doom to you who think you're so smart,
who hold such a high opinion of yourselves!
All you're good at is drinking—champion boozers
who collect trophies from drinking bouts
And then line your pockets with bribes from the guilty
while you violate the rights of the innocent.

ISAIAH 5:18-23

Are we so different? When we subtly give in to idolatry, worshiping in place of God that which is not God, don't we get self-absorbed and forget about our neighbors and those in need? Israel and Judah have been puffed up with pride here, and the Lord calls them "champion boozers" who take bribes and stomp all over the innocent. Lord, have mercy!

Take a moment to reflect on the following questions.

4. What emotions are communicated in this poem?

5. What sins of injustice are described in the passage?

6. How would you describe idolatry in your own words?

7. Why does idolatry inevitably lead to injustice?

8. In what ways does Jesus lead us into proper love for God (worship) and proper love for neighbor (justice)?

The Neighborhood

Justice is a Jesus-informed virtue. In loving Jesus, we are among those who ache for the world to be made right. In our modern times, we have access (via social media and other digital forms of communication) to see injustice not only in our neighborhoods but also in hundreds and hundreds of neighborhoods around the world. Our digital proximity to atrocities, war, suffering, and injustices around the world can be overwhelming, because while we have near limitless access to learn about these tragedies, we have very limited ability to do anything about them.

The beauty of the diversity of the body of Christ is that God gives us different justice burdens. (A justice burden is a unique sensitivity toward some form of injustice.) Some may be drawn toward people experiencing poverty or homelessness. Others may be burdened by racial injustice, at-risk youth, or domestic-abuse survivors. Some may feel for undocumented immigrants among us or incarcerated men and women. Our responsibility is to start in prayer, respond to the justice burdens God has given us, and look in our neighborhoods to see what we are able to do.

9. What is one injustice you are particularly burdened about?

10. What could you do to be part of God's work of justice in your neighborhood, community, or city?

The Prayer

With thoughts of justice on your mind, offer this prayer.

O God, you have made us in your image to be a people of worship and justice. Where we have failed to love you, have mercy on us. Where we have failed to love our neighbors as ourselves, have mercy on us. We long to work with you in setting right what has gone wrong in your good world. Guide us by the Holy Spirit to be aware of the injustices around us, and empower us by the same Spirit to be the justice bringers in our neighborhoods. It's all for Christ's sake we pray. Amen.

LESSON 4

A VIRGIN WILL GET PREGNANT

The Approach

I believe all pregnant women deserve a nine-month pass.

While life is growing in their bodies, I'm advocating for them to receive a universally recognized pass to do pretty much whatever they want to do—without judgment. If they want to eat ice cream and pickles for lunch, so be it. If they would rather stay home and call upon other family members to run errands, then their family should enthusiastically go when asked. If they would like first choice on movie night for the entire nine months of their pregnancy, I say, hand over the remote control.

My wife asked for very little during our three pregnancies. (I say "*our* pregnancies" as if I had much to do with it. She was the one carrying each of our children in her womb!) She did regularly request Tater Tots during the first pregnancy because for the first few months those little processed potato cylinders were just about all she could keep down. She remained active during all the pregnancies, hardly slowing down, even when her legs began to swell and her ankles disappeared during her last one. We were teaching a Bible class for fourth and fifth graders during that last pregnancy, and one of the boys, who we knew well, pointed at my wife's swollen ankles and said, "Mrs. Jenni, your legs look like a beluga whale!" That boy could have kept his comment to himself, but he didn't. My wife and I both laughed. We still laugh when we tell that story.

Pregnancy features prominently in the Jesus story because Jesus' mom became pregnant in the most unexpected way. Mary, the mother of Jesus, conceived the Word of God by the power of the Holy Spirit. Mary and Joseph were headed toward matrimony, but their marriage had not yet been consummated. Mary received a visit from an angel named Gabriel, who said, "Mary, you have nothing to fear. God has a surprise for you: You will become pregnant and give birth to a son and call his name Jesus" (Luke 1:30-31). Shocked but receptive to this message from heaven, Mary would go on to become the mother of Jesus and receive perpetual respect as the Blessed Virgin Mary.

Her mysterious pregnancy came about as the fulfillment of a prophecy from Isaiah uttered more than five hundred years previously, during the reign of King Ahaz of Judah, who sat on the throne during the time of the divided kingdom. As I mentioned earlier, Judah was the southern kingdom, the counterpart to the northern kingdom, which was called Israel. The kings of Judah reigned from Jerusalem while the kings of Israel held a throne in Samaria.

Like many kings of Israel and Judah, Ahaz did evil in the sight of the Lord. He wasn't remembered kindly:

> Ahaz was twenty years old when he became king and he ruled for sixteen years in Jerusalem. He didn't behave in the eyes of his God; he wasn't at all like his ancestor David. Instead he followed in the track of the kings of Israel. He even indulged in the outrageous practice of "passing his son through the fire"—a truly abominable act he picked up from the pagans God had earlier thrown out of the country. He also participated in the activities of the neighborhood sex-and-religion shrines that flourished all over the place.
>
> 2 KINGS 16:2-4

Fear overtakes Ahaz during his reign because the king of Syria and the king of Israel join forces and plan to attack Judah. The prophet Isaiah shows up on Ahaz's doorstep with a message of hope. He told Ahaz not to worry—the Syrian and Israelite armies were not going to attack. (Little did Ahaz know it would be the Assyrians attacking instead—see Isaiah 8:5-8.)

In the midst of Isaiah's reassurance, God showed up to Ahaz: "God spoke again to Ahaz. This time he said, 'Ask for a sign from your God. Ask anything. Be extravagant. Ask for the moon!' But Ahaz said, 'I'd never do that. I'd never make demands like that on God!'" (Isaiah 7:10-12). We can only speculate at Ahaz's tone, but it appears that Ahaz was not being sincere. He probably didn't want a sign from God because that would obligate him to be obedient to God. King Ahaz wasn't walking in the ways of King David who, as flawed as he was, attempted to lead with uprightness of heart (see Psalm 78:70-72). When David had sinned, he had repented. While King David had a heart in pursuit of God's justice and righteousness, Ahaz followed the desires of his own heart, one that had been corrupted by the influence of Judah's pagan neighbors.

Before we dive in and explore the sign given to King Ahaz, take a moment to reflect on the following questions.

1. Who do you know who has had a difficult pregnancy?

2. What are some of the best ways to show a pregnant woman kindness and respect?

3. If you could ask God for a sign, what would that sign look like?

The Word

Ahaz and the kings of Israel hadn't treated God well. As we have seen, God planted Israel and Judah into fertile soil to be a vineyard of righteousness and justice. They were the people of the one true Creator-God, the people God had worked to fashion into a community of worship and justice. God wanted Israel and Judah to be "a light for the *nations*" so that God's saving power would become a global experience (Isaiah 49:6). Ahaz spuriously rejected God's request to ask for a sign, but God gave Ahaz a sign anyway, through the mouthpiece of Isaiah the prophet.

The prophetic message from God to Ahaz would come to have a dual fulfillment, as is the case with many Old Testament prophecies. Another example of dual fulfillment is found when Peter quotes from Joel 2:28-32 in his sermon on the Day of Pentecost (see Acts 2:14-21). God poured out the Spirit on all kinds of people at Pentecost, but the promised Judgment Day, what Peter calls "the Day of the Lord" (Acts 2:20), had yet to come. That day is still in front of us. The Day of God's Judgment, which is referenced throughout the Old Testament, will be the time when God will come to reign as King, Judge, and Savior.

God's prophetic word given to King Ahaz would have dual fulfillment, but first it begins with a sign:

> Isaiah told him, "Then listen to this, government of David! It's bad enough that you make people tired with your pious, timid hypocrisies, but now you're making God tired. So the Master is going to give you a sign anyway. Watch for this: A girl who is presently a virgin will get pregnant. She'll bear a son and name him Immanuel (God-With-Us)."
>
> ISAIAH 7:13-14

Jesus is God-With-Us. He came into the world as a sign of God's love for the entire world. Jesus is the Word made flesh and blood, who lived among us *as us*, revealing God's neighboring presence among us. Jesus is the latter fulfillment of this prophecy. The earlier fulfillment was to come in the lifetime of King Ahaz: A woman who would give birth in the days of King Ahaz would name her child Immanuel, and before the child was an adult, the threat of war from Israel and Syria would be no more!

> [Isaiah said,] "By the time the child is twelve years old, able to make moral decisions, the threat of war will be over. Relax, those two kings that have you so worried will be out of the picture. But also be warned: God will bring on you and your people and your government a judgment worse than anything since the time the kingdom split, when Ephraim left Judah. The king of Assyria is coming!"
>
> ISAIAH 7:15-17

Judgment—coming in the form of the Assyrian army, which plays out in Isaiah 8—was the first fulfillment. The second fulfillment, the one we are most interested in, took place hundreds of years later with the birth of Jesus. Look at how Matthew shows the latter, second fulfillment of Isaiah's virgin prophecy:

> While [Joseph] was trying to figure a way out [of being engaged to Mary], he had a dream. God's angel spoke in the dream: "Joseph, son of David, don't hesitate to get married. Mary's pregnancy is Spirit-conceived. God's Holy Spirit has made her pregnant. She will bring a son to birth, and when she does, you, Joseph, will name him Jesus—'God saves'—because he will save his people from their sins." This would bring the prophet's embryonic revelation to full term:
>
> Watch for this—a virgin will get pregnant and bear a son;
> They will name him Immanuel (Hebrew for "God is with us").
>
> MATTHEW 1:20-23

The Holy Spirit, who hovered over the uncreated earth "like a bird above the watery abyss" (Genesis 1:2), hovered over Mary, conceiving a child. The angel instructed Joseph to give the child a name that means "God saves." Notice the pregnancy imagery near the end of Matthew 1. Mary's pregnancy took Isaiah's "embryonic revelation to full term" so that the prophecy of Isaiah might be born into the world! Jesus came to us as the God who saves by being with us.

This single revelation fulfilled in Jesus is foundational:

- *God-With-Us* is at the heart of the Christmas story.
- *God-With-Us* is the essence of the gospel.
- *God-With-Us* reveals the nature and vocation of Jesus.
- *God-With-Us* is the source of our faith, hope, and love.

Mary's role in all this cannot be overstated. When she discovered that her cousin Elizabeth was six months pregnant, she ran to tell Elizabeth the good news of her own pregnancy. When Elizabeth greeted Mary, the baby in Elizabeth's womb leapt for joy! Elizabeth exclaimed,

> You're so blessed among women,
> and the babe in your womb, also blessed! . . .
> Blessed woman, who believed what God said,
> believed every word would come true!
>
> LUKE 1:42, 45

We call Mary blessed because of these words. Catholic and some Protestant Christians have the tradition of calling her the Blessed Virgin Mary. Protestants don't believe she remained a virgin for the rest of her life, but all Christians believe she was a virgin at the birth of Jesus. We all believe the words of Elizabeth that Mary was blessed in her humble acceptance of what the angel had spoken to her regarding her virgin conception.

Mary has been honored in the church from nearly the beginning. Irenaeus, a second-century church father, describes Mary as the "cause of salvation, both to herself and the whole human race."[1] Her words of consent to God's message via the angel Gabriel—"Let it be with me / just as you say" (Luke 1:38)—became the mainspring by which salvation came.

Similarly to how Paul describes Jesus as the second Adam (see Romans 5:12-21), Irenaeus describes Mary as the second Eve: "The knot of Eve's disobedience was loosed by the obedience of Mary. For what the virgin Eve had bound fast through unbelief, this did the virgin Mary set free through faith."[2] Mary came to undo Eve's tragic mistake. Reflect for a moment on this crayon-and-pencil drawing from Sister Grace Remington of the Sisters of the Mississippi Abbey.

Mary is the Blessed Virgin and the new Eve. Notice how Eve, with the snake curled around her leg and fruit in her hand, looks with regret as she touches Mary's pregnant belly. Notice Mary, with her foot on the head of the snake, looking at Eve with an expression of hope.

Mary isn't the Savior; she gave birth to the Savior. We don't worship Mary, because worship belongs to God alone; we worship her son. But we do honor Mary by imitating her faith and obedience.

Take a moment to reflect on the following questions.

4. Pause and think about the miracle of God-With-Us, God who has moved into our neighborhood in the person of Jesus. How does that make you feel?

5. If you were Mary, how would you have reacted if you learned you were pregnant while still a virgin?

6. If you were Joseph, how would you have felt hearing from an angel that this virgin birth would come about by the Holy Spirit?

7. In what ways is Mary the new Eve? How did Mary undo the knots created by Eve?

8. What emotions arise as you consider the drawing of Mary and Eve? Hope? Grief? Take some time to name those feelings.

The Neighborhood

As Protestants, we don't pray *to* Mary, but we do pray *with* Mary. In her meeting with Elizabeth, Mary breaks out in prayer in the form of a song. Mary's song, traditionally called the Magnificat, is filled with prophetic power and prayer for our neighborhoods:

> I'm bursting with God-news;
>   I'm dancing the song of my Savior God.
> God took one good look at me, and look what happened—
>   I'm the most fortunate woman on earth!
> What God has done for me will never be forgotten,
>   the God whose very name is holy, set apart from all others.
> His mercy flows in wave after wave
>   on those who are in awe before him.

He bared his arm and showed his strength,
    scattered the bluffing braggarts.
He knocked tyrants off their high horses,
    pulled victims out of the mud.
The starving poor sat down to a banquet;
    the callous rich were left out in the cold.
He embraced his chosen child, Israel;
    he remembered and piled on the mercies, piled them high.
It's exactly what he promised,
    beginning with Abraham and right up to now.

LUKE 1:46-55

With Mary's song in your mind, consider these questions.

9. Who are the "victims" in your neighborhood or city who need to be "pulled . . . out of the mud"? How could you help them?

10. Who are the “starving poor” near you? What would loving them look like?

The Prayer

With Mary’s prophetic song stirring your imagination, offer this prayer.

Savior-God, we worship you as the one who comes to rescue and save. Thank you for coming to us. Thank you for joining us in the humanity of your dear Son. Thank you for your neighboring presence among us. May your presence embolden us to reach out toward those in need, to lend a helpful hand of hospitality. May we live with the kind of faith we see in the Blessed Virgin Mary. All for your name’s sake, amen.

LESSON 5

A CHILD HAS BEEN BORN FOR US

The Approach

I love the Christmas season because Christmas provides space to rediscover the childhood wonder and magic often forgotten by adults.

I love the parties, the music, the movies, the family gatherings, the Christmas cookies, the Christmas cards, and the Christmas trees. I never grow tired of the lights outside our house in November and the candlelight inside our church on Christmas Eve. I treasure all the traditions that coalesce in our annual celebration of the birth of Jesus. With much sadness, I've noticed a growing disdain for Christmas decorations that go up before Thanksgiving and the four Sundays of Advent. It's as if the spirit of Ebenezer Scrooge—that "bah humbug" spirit—has settled into the hearts of some people. Some people dislike the improper timing of pre-Thanksgiving Christmas decorations. Others weary of the commercialization of Christmas.

But there's no need to fret! Christmas traditions are just that—traditions to be adapted, not rules etched in stone. We hold the celebration of the birth of Jesus in such high esteem that we put forth effort for weeks (and sometimes months!) in advance to prepare. Perhaps the "bah humbug" spirit can be cast out when we see decorations going up in November and hear Christmas music at Thanksgiving as the sights and sounds of preparation.

Christmas remains the annual reminder that some things are still sacred. In our high-paced, commodified world, where many are enslaved by "the economy," I find it interesting that most retail stores still close on Christmas Day. It seems that in a symbolic way even big-box department stores may bow their knees in an act of worship before the newborn King. Certainly, Christmas has become a worldwide celebration by Christians and non-Christians alike. Not everyone enters the sacredness of the season, acknowledging the miracle of God-With-Us, God moving into our neighborhood. But Christmas at least gives the world the opportunity to stop and wonder.

We celebrate Christmas during some of the shortest days of the year, when the pervasive darkness of night seems unending. Imagine flickering Christmas lights glowing in a dark cul-de-sac absent of the sun. Or picture vivid Christmas-tree lights illuminating a darkened living room. These lights penetrating the darkness inspire a sense of awe. They provide time and space to wonder if perhaps this disenchanted world of work and woe has only been eclipsing a larger world of grace and godliness.

We are returning to Isaiah in this lesson to look at the words of the prophet in chapter 9. Christmas cards often draw upon these well-known words from Isaiah 9:6 (KJV):

> Unto us a child is born, unto us a son is given:
> and the government shall be upon his shoulder:
> and his name shall be called Wonderful, Counsellor,
> The mighty God,
> The everlasting Father,
> The Prince of Peace.

The Word who moved into our neighborhood is our wonderful Counselor, the embodiment of the mighty God, the everlasting father of a new humanity, and the Prince of Peace leading us in the ways of peace.

Before we take a deep dive into this section of Isaiah, take a moment to reflect on these questions.

1. Do you send out Christmas cards? Why or why not?

2. What are some of the ways you make space for sacredness during the Christmas season?

3. What do Christmas decorations look like at your house? When do you start the decorating process?

The Word

More important than providing cheery language for Christmas cards, the sacred words of Isaiah 9:6 form a connection between the Hebrew Prophets and the birth of Jesus, between the Old Testament and the New Testament, between the old covenant and the new covenant. Out of all the Gospel writers, Matthew in particular seems interested in making this connection between the prophecies in Isaiah and their fulfillment in Jesus. As we saw in the previous lesson, Matthew 1:23 connects back to Isaiah 7:14:

> The birth of Jesus took place like this. His mother, Mary, was engaged to be married to Joseph. Before they enjoyed their wedding night, Joseph discovered she was pregnant. (It was by the Holy Spirit, but he didn't know that.) Joseph, chagrined but noble, determined to take care of things quietly so Mary would not be disgraced.
>
> While he was trying to figure a way out, he had a dream. God's angel spoke in the dream: "Joseph, son of David, don't hesitate to get married. Mary's pregnancy is Spirit-conceived. God's Holy Spirit has made her pregnant. She will bring a son to birth, and when she does, you, Joseph, will name him Jesus—'God saves'—because

he will save his people from their sins." This would bring the prophet's embryonic revelation to full term:

> Watch for this—a virgin will get pregnant and bear a son;
> They will name him Immanuel (Hebrew for "God is with us").

MATTHEW 1:18-23

Joseph discovered that Mary was pregnant before they got married. *The Message* notably describes him as "chagrined but noble." He probably felt embarrassed, but Joseph, being a man of high moral character, didn't want Mary to be shamed, so he planned to break things off with her quietly—until an angel appeared to him and explained what was going on: The birth of Jesus would fulfill what Isaiah prophesied (in Isaiah 7) about a virgin bearing a son.

Matthew 3 gives us another example of Matthew drawing connections between Isaiah's prophecies—this time from Isaiah 40:3—and Jesus' birth:

While Jesus was living in the Galilean hills, John, called "the Baptizer," was preaching in the desert country of Judea. His message was simple and austere, like his desert surroundings: "Change your life. God's kingdom is here."

John and his message were authorized by Isaiah's prophecy:

> Thunder in the desert!
> Prepare for God's arrival!
> Make the road smooth and straight!

John dressed in a camel-hair habit tied at the waist by a leather strap. He lived on a diet of locusts and wild field honey. People poured out of Jerusalem, Judea, and the Jordanian countryside to hear and see him in action. There at the Jordan River those who came to confess their sins were baptized into a changed life.

MATTHEW 3:1-6

Jesus began his earthly ministry by being baptized by John, aptly called the Baptizer. John's mom, Elizabeth, had been pregnant for six months when Mary discovered her own pregnancy. In our last lesson, we learned Elizabeth and Mary were cousins, making John and Jesus relatives too. Elizabeth is the one who said to Mary, "You're so blessed among women, / and the babe in your womb, also blessed!" (Luke 1:42). John the Baptizer came preparing the way for Jesus, and his entire ministry fulfilled what Isaiah says in Isaiah 40:3.

Finally, we see the words in Matthew 4 connecting back to Isaiah's prophecy recorded in Isaiah 9. Matthew writes,

> When Jesus got word that John had been arrested, he returned to Galilee. He moved from his hometown, Nazareth, to the lakeside village Capernaum, nestled at the base of the Zebulun and Naphtali hills. This move completed Isaiah's revelation:
>
> Land of Zebulun, land of Naphtali,
> road to the sea, over Jordan,
> Galilee, crossroads for the nations.
> People sitting out their lives in the dark
> saw a huge light;
> Sitting in that dark, dark country of death,
> they watched the sun come up.
>
> This Isaiah-prophesied revelation came to life in Galilee the moment Jesus started preaching. He picked up where John left off: "Change your life. God's kingdom is here."
>
> MATTHEW 4:12-17

Jesus grew up in Galilee, an area known as the "crossroads for the nations" or as some translations, like the ESV and KJV, put it, "Galilee of the Gentiles" (Matthew 4:15). Jesus called his disciples from this part of ancient Israel. This northern area was primarily occupied by non-Jewish (i.e., Gentile) inhabitants. Many other people from various nations traveled through this area, making it a major thoroughfare. Jewish people, like the people in Jesus' family, were living in that area in the darkness of their pagan neighbors, but according to Isaiah, the hope was that they would see a great light. Jesus moved into the neighborhood as the Light of the World, a light for the Gentile nations. Jesus came to fulfill Isaiah's prophecy.

Notice the language in Matthew's Gospel regarding the activity around Jesus' birth and life:

- "This would bring the prophet's embryonic revelation to full term" (1:22).
- "This move completed Isaiah's revelation" (4:14).
- "This Isaiah-prophesied revelation came to life" (4:17).

Jesus didn't come to abolish the Old Testament Law and Prophets but to *fulfill* them. Jesus was Israel-in-person in that he summed up the identity and mission of both Israel and Judah. In doing so, Jesus did for Israel and Judah what they could not do for themselves. We need the Old Testament to help us make sense of the New Testament. We need Isaiah to understand Jesus. With that in mind, let's dive into this important passage in Isaiah 9.

> There'll be no darkness for those who were in trouble. Earlier he did bring the lands of Zebulun and Naphtali into disrepute, but the time is coming when he'll make that whole area glorious—the road along the Sea, the country past the Jordan, international Galilee.
>
> ISAIAH 9:1

Zebulun and Naphtali were two of the northernmost tribes in Israel. As mentioned above, Jesus grew up in this area. People from this region were known as Galileans because of their geographic proximity to the Sea of Galilee. The people of that region had been living in darkness, which may have been a self-imposed darkness brought by their accommodation of pagan ideas from the large number of non-Jewish people living there.

> The people who walked in darkness
>   have seen a great light.
> For those who lived in a land of deep shadows—
>   light! sunbursts of light!
> You repopulated the nation,
>   you expanded its joy.
> Oh, they're so glad in your presence!
>   Festival joy!
> The joy of a great celebration,
>   sharing rich gifts and warm greetings.
>
> ISAIAH 9:2-3

Notice the contrast between light and darkness in these words. These northern tribes have been living in darkness, but "sunbursts of light" will arrive with joy in their rays. Many people, myself included, suffer from seasonal depression when it is dark and cloudy for days and days, but we know the joy that comes on that first sunny day in spring!

> The abuse of oppressors and cruelty of tyrants—
>   all their whips and clubs and curses—
> Is gone, done away with, a deliverance
>   as surprising and sudden as Gideon's old victory over Midian.
> The boots of all those invading troops,
>   along with their shirts soaked with innocent blood,
> Will be piled in a heap and burned,
>   a fire that will burn for days!
>
> ISAIAH 9:4-5

Liberation amplifies the joy with the arrival of light! These verses reverberate with the hope of freedom from oppressors and the end of fighting as the uniforms of the invading army will be used for firewood. Here Isaiah is echoing the "playing war no more" sentiment from a few lessons back.

> For a child has been born—for us!
>   the gift of a son—for us!
> He'll take over
>   the running of the world.
> His names will be: Amazing Counselor,
>   Strong God,
> Eternal Father,
>   Prince of Wholeness.
> His ruling authority will grow,
>   and there'll be no limits to the wholeness he brings.
> He'll rule from the historic David throne
>   over that promised kingdom.
> He'll put that kingdom on a firm footing
>   and keep it going
> With fair dealing and right living,
>   beginning now and lasting always.
> The zeal of God-of-the-Angel-Armies
>   will do all this.
>
> ISAIAH 9:6-7

A son would be born, the Messiah, the Jewish King who would come from the royal lineage of King David. There would be no end to the wholeness and peace he'd bring, because he would be the Prince of *Wholeness*, a good English translation of the Hebrew word *shalom*, meaning "peace" and "well-being." He would be the light in their darkness, the liberation for their captivity, and the fair dealing to replace their oppression. Jesus is that King.

Take a moment to reflect on the following questions.

4. How do you find the Old Testament in general? Confusing? Boring? Unimportant? Fascinating? Hopeful? Interesting? Too weird? Too daunting?

5. What are some of the things we can do to connect the Old Testament to our reading of the New Testament?

6. How do the images of darkness and light affect how you think of the birth of Jesus, the Word who moved into our neighborhood?

7. What does this passage communicate to you about Jesus as Lord, Savior, and King?

8. Which of the four names given in the passage above—Amazing Counselor, Strong God, Eternal Father, Prince of Wholeness—speaks to you the most today?

The Neighborhood

Let's shift from a reflection on the names given to Jesus and what they mean to a consideration of what these four names reveal to us about Jesus at work in our neighborhoods. The language from the King James Version of Isaiah 9:6 has been used so often that for many the words have lost their imaginative power. The fresh language in *The Message* offers us the opportunity to gain new insights. Let's begin by comparing *The Message* translation with the King James translation.

Names for God in Isaiah 9:6

The Message	King James
Amazing Counselor	Wonderful, Counsellor
Strong God	Mighty God
Eternal Father	Everlasting Father
Prince of Wholeness	Prince of Peace

Jesus embodies all the wisdom of God. He is our trustworthy and reliable Counselor. Do people in our neighborhoods see us followers of Jesus as reliable counselors?

Jesus is God, the Strong God. In the words of the Nicene Creed, Jesus is "true God from true God." He moved into our neighborhood so we could truly see the heart and nature of God.

Jesus is not God the Father; he is the Son. However, he is the father of a new humanity, the firstborn of all creation. He shows those of us in the neighborhood how to be human.

And Jesus is our peace, cultivating well-being and human flourishing in our communities.

9. What can you do to grow in Jesus-centered wisdom, to be a voice of counsel and help to those around you?

10. What can you do to embody the wholeness and peace Jesus came to bring to the world?

The Prayer

As you live in the light brought by King Jesus in his incarnation and birth, offer this prayer.

King Jesus, shine the light of your love in our hearts and in the heart of our neighborhood. Show yourself to be our Amazing Counselor to rescue those drowning in folly. Show yourself to be the Strong God to those suffering in weakness. Show yourself to be the Eternal Father, guiding people into fulfilling lives. Show yourself to be the Prince of Wholeness to those who are broken. For the sake of your name, amen.

LESSON 6

MESSIAH AND MASTER

The Approach

I can't imagine *not* celebrating my birthday every year, even though we live in a culture that's averse to aging.

It's not just a secular phenomenon: Too many people—both inside and outside the church—stop acknowledging their age when they reach a certain year. Some people want to hold on to twenty-nine or thirty-nine or forty-nine forever. Not me. I want to live in the moment, marking each birthday as it comes. For my thirtieth birthday, I had a big cookout at my house with many of my friends. Some of the teenagers from my youth group crashed the party, which I loved! For my fortieth birthday, I concluded a multiday hike on the Appalachian Trail in Georgia with my brother and a mutual friend. For my fiftieth birthday, I ran a half-marathon along the Missouri River just north of Kansas City. Who knows what I will do for my sixtieth birthday!

Birthdays not only give us the opportunity to *be* celebrated, they also provide a catalyst *to* celebrate the people in our lives. A birthday celebration invites us to share the things we feel but rarely say to the one blowing out the candles. When we celebrate a friend on their birthday with time, a gift, a card, or even a simple text message, we communicate to them their worth and value to us.

Every birthday presents us with a break from the monotony of our day-to-day lives, a welcome pause from the immediate and mundane. Many of us get busy with work and family and our ever-growing to-do lists. Birthdays create space for an annual celebration. Our birthdays give us a special opportunity to look up and be grateful for the gift of being, the gift of life itself. I have joked with my children that my birthday is *almost* the most important day of the year, second only to the ultimate birthday celebration that comes around every year on December 25.

Christmas remains the most significant date on my calendar even if some people don't acknowledge—or perhaps even know—what it means. For those of us who believe in Jesus, Christmas marks the day of the birth of the newborn King, born in Bethlehem, adored by shepherds, worshiped by angels, feared by an evil king, and loved by a peasant family—a birthday like none other! The Word moved in and took residence, not in a palace or the home of a noble family but in the flesh of a baby boy wrapped in swaddling clothes and laid in a manger.

Matthew's Gospel gives us the account of the angelic visitor in Joseph's dream and the visit of the wise men from the East, whereas Mark records nothing about the birth of Jesus. John gives only a passing reference to the birth of Jesus but makes the beautiful proclamation that Jesus, the Word of God, has taken on flesh and blood and "moved into the neighborhood" (John 1:14). Luke's Gospel offers the most details about this sacred event—the decree from Emperor Augustus, the lack of room in the inn, the messenger angels, the angelic choir, the manger, and Mary, who "treasured up all these things, pondering them in her heart" (Luke 2:19, ESV). The angels proclaimed that the one born that day was "Christ the Lord" (Luke 2:11, KJV), translated in *The Message* appropriately, and with some alliteration, as "Messiah and Master."

Before we walk through the Christmas story in Luke 2, reflect on the following questions.

1. What is one of your most memorable birthdays? What did you do on that day to celebrate?

2. When you let your mind wonder, what do you daydream about?

3. Did you grow up celebrating Christmas? If so, what is your favorite Christmas memory from childhood? If not, what do you recall your neighbors doing to celebrate Christmas?

The Word

Many of us who have grown up in the church are most familiar with the Luke 2 Christmas story in the language of the King James Version. For me, it's nostalgic to hear the opening of the Christmas story with the words "It came to pass in those days, that there went out a decree from Caesar Augustus that all the world should be taxed" (Luke 2:1, KJV). Using this translation for worship on Christmas Eve or during worship on the first Sunday after Christmas Day makes a lot of sense. But for Bible study I find great value in reading this passage in various translations. *The Message* translation will, at times, sound a bit different if you read it out loud, but let those differences stir your curiosity.

> About that time Caesar Augustus ordered a census to be taken throughout the Empire. This was the first census when Quirinius was governor of Syria. Everyone had to travel to his own ancestral hometown to be accounted for. So Joseph went from the Galilean town of Nazareth up to Bethlehem in Judah, David's town, for

> the census. As a descendant of David, he had to go there. He went with Mary, his fiancée, who was pregnant.
>
> LUKE 2:1-5

Nazareth was Jesus' hometown. He would grow up in that Galilean town after a short excursion with his family to Egypt. But Jesus' parents traveled to Bethlehem for his birth. This place confirmed the prophetic message from Micah: "But you, Bethlehem, David's country, / the runt of the litter— / From you will come the leader / who will shepherd-rule Israel. / He'll be no upstart, no pretender. / His family tree is ancient and distinguished" (Micah 5:2). A Ruler, the one who would rule like David, in the family lineage of David, would be born in Bethlehem.

> While they were there, the time came for [Mary] to give birth. She gave birth to a son, her firstborn. She wrapped him in a blanket and laid him in a manger, because there was no room in the hostel.
>
> LUKE 2:6-7

Mary would go on to have other children, but Jesus was her firstborn son. For those of us who have children, it seems like no matter how much we prepare we are never quite ready for the birth of our firstborns. When my first child was born, I thought I was ready because I had read a stack of books on babies and parenting. While I had picked up some helpful information from my reading, nothing fully prepared me for the moment I held my firstborn son in my arms. I suppose Mary felt some of the same things I did. The "swaddling clothes" she wrapped Jesus in (Luke 2:7, KJV) were nothing more than an ordinary blanket. She laid him in a manger, a feeding trough for animals. There was nothing extraordinary about Jesus' birth at this point—nothing extraordinary *yet.*

> There were shepherds camping in the neighborhood. They had set night watches over their sheep. Suddenly, God's angel stood among them and God's glory

> blazed around them. They were terrified. The angel said, "Don't be afraid. I'm here to announce a great and joyful event that is meant for everybody, worldwide: A Savior has just been born in David's town, a Savior who is Messiah and Master. This is what you're to look for: a baby wrapped in a blanket and lying in a manger."
>
> LUKE 2:8-12

The blanket, and even the manger, were commonplace items in first-century Jewish homes, but the birth of Jesus took a turn toward the dramatic when God's angel showed up at night amid a group of shepherds camping in the neighborhood. The angelic messenger announced the birth of not an ordinary child but a Savior!

The angel described the infant Savior as both Messiah and Master. The English words *Christ* and *Messiah* are anglicized versions of the word *christos* (Greek) and the word *mashiach* (Hebrew). Both terms mean "anointed one," often in reference to a king. The word for the anointed Jewish King is *Messiah.* The Savior-King would be the Lord *and* Master. He would be in charge of the people of God. Jesus, our Messiah and Master.

> At once the angel was joined by a huge angelic choir singing God's praises:
>
> Glory to God in the heavenly heights,
> Peace to all men and women on earth who please him.
>
> LUKE 2:13-14

A choir of angels worshiping God joined the messenger angel, celebrating the birth of the Messiah and Master. They directed their praise to heaven—to the God of glory. The overflow of their praise sent blessings down to earth, predominantly the blessing of peace. As we saw in the previous lesson, that peace is the Hebrew concept of *shalom*, meaning well-being or wholeness. The Messiah and Master would come to Israel as the "Prince of Wholeness" (Isaiah 9:6), and "his government and its peace / will never end" (Isaiah 9:7, NLT).

> As the angel choir withdrew into heaven, the shepherds talked it over. "Let's get over to Bethlehem *as fast as we can* and see for ourselves what God has revealed to us." They left, *running*, and found Mary and Joseph, and the baby lying in the manger. Seeing was believing. They told everyone they met what the angels had said about this child. All who heard the shepherds were impressed.
>
> LUKE 2:15-18 (EMPHASIS ADDED)

The shepherds, excited by the angelic messenger and choir performance, ran to see the baby Jesus for themselves. They did not walk—*they ran!* For these Jewish shepherds, the joy of the Savior's birth flowed from the hope that Jesus would be the Messiah and Master who would redeem Israel. They ran with unbridled joy and expectant hope that Jesus would be the one to rescue them from the cruel oppression of the Romans and restore Moses' vision of a people known for worship and justice. When they saw the newborn Jesus, the Word of God in flesh and blood, they believed. For the shepherds, "seeing was [indeed] believing."

> Mary kept all these things to herself, holding them dear, deep within herself. The shepherds returned and let loose, glorifying and praising God for everything they had heard and seen. It turned out exactly the way they'd been told!
>
> LUKE 2:19-20

The shepherds returned to their sheep in the exuberance of the moment. Their worship was uninhibited. They "let loose" in authentic shouts and prayers of thanksgiving, for the King had come.

Mary's reaction was less animated and more introspective. She stored up all these events in her heart. She meditated deeply on the significance of the moment. We can expect vocal songs of joy at the arrival of Jesus, but Mary shows us the equally valuable way to respond to the Messiah and Master. Inner transformation occurs through quiet meditation and reflection.

Following Mary's lead, reflect on the following questions.

4. What are some differences between reading a book about babies and actually holding a baby in your arms?

5. At the heart of the gospel story is Jesus as King, born to rule as Israel's Messiah and the world's true Master and Lord. Why do we need a King?

6. What is your favorite Christmas song? Do you like traditional Christmas carols, modern Christmas songs, or both?

7. How do you think you would have responded if you were in Bethlehem for that first Christmas morning? Would you have been more like the shepherds or more like Mary?

8. Mary the mother of Jesus continues to be a model for us, not only in her faith and obedience but also in her practice of meditation. Pause for a moment and meditate on the utter mystery of the Son of God taking on human flesh and blood to be our Savior, Messiah, and Master. What thoughts or feelings come to mind?

The Neighborhood

The Christmas celebration remains a public holiday in the Western world, certainly in the United States, even if many of our non-Christian neighbors pay more attention to Santa Claus than Jesus. What can we do to shine the light of Jesus in our neighborhoods during Christmastide? My approach is not to argue for anti-Santa rhetoric or guilt-ridden signs about Jesus being the real "reason for the season." Rather, I agree with my friend Rich Villodas, who writes, "I get the idea of keeping Christ in Christmas, but I'm more concerned about keeping Christ in Christians."[1] What can we do to allow the joy of Jesus' birth to be so alive in our hearts that it overflows into our neighborhoods and workplaces? There's no joy to be found in rebuking our non-Christian neighbors for not acting like Jesus, but perhaps we can trust the Spirit to form Christ within us at Christmas.

9. What are some practical ways you can demonstrate Christmas joy where you live?

10. Who in your community is overlooked or forgotten at Christmastime? What can you do to acknowledge and love them?

The Prayer

As you reflect on the joy celebrated during the season of Christmas, offer this prayer.

God of all power and might, the source of every perfect gift, thank you for sending us the gift of your Son. May we receive Jesus as Messiah and Master today and every day. Send us your Holy Spirit. May we be known not for what we are against but for the love and joy emanating from us. We offer ourselves to you in faith and action. Have mercy on us in the name of Jesus. Amen.

LESSON 7

THE WORD IN THE NEIGHBORHOOD

The Approach

I grew up in a quaint neighborhood in a midsize Midwestern town.

While I was born in Alabama and spent a good portion of my early childhood living throughout the Gulf Coast region, I spent my later childhood and all my adolescent years in the Midwest. The neighborhood we moved into when I was ten years old was marked at the entrance with a short brick wall with iron letters. Myrna Manor North was a small neighborhood of nondescript homes with two-car garages and duplexes primarily rented out to families with small children. It seemed like every other driveway had a basketball hoop ready for pickup games year-round. At the north end of the neighborhood sat a small wooded area, which covered a creek that ran a mile or so to the 102 River. I have many fond memories of that creek, those woods, and that neighborhood, which was filled with activity, particularly in the summer. The many kids near my age in Myrna Manor North and I would play hide-and-seek on endless summer days. As I got older, I would mow lawns for my neighbors during the day and sit in friends' driveways listening to the radio as the stars came out.

Our neighbors didn't lock their doors. (Maybe some of them did. I never checked to see.) We all knew everyone in our community by name, including Mr. George, our next-door neighbor, who was a quiet man who mostly kept to himself. He'd wave when he was working in his yard as we drove by. He gave me a surprisingly large cash gift when I graduated high school even though I had only spoken to him a couple of times. This idyllic neighborhood was home to the kind of people who would loan you a cup of sugar when you were out or shovel the snow from your driveway if you were unable. It was an average, white, middle-class, Midwestern neighborhood. I could never have imagined what it would have looked like if God had moved into *our* neighborhood.

This historical event—Jesus as God-With-Us in human flesh—is what theologians call the incarnation. The God of creation took up residence with the creatures God had made. The God of heaven made his dwelling with the people of earth. God's neighboring presence with us is one of the predominant themes of the story the Bible tells. We stumble upon references to the presence of God-With-Us throughout the Bible:

- God walked with Adam in the garden of Eden (Genesis 3:8).
- God spoke to Hagar through an angel while she suffered mistreatment (Genesis 16:7-12).
- God was with Abraham when he made a covenant with him (Genesis 17:1-22).
- God was with Isaac in Beersheba (Genesis 26:19-24).
- God was with Jacob when he dreamed of the ladder ascending into heaven (Genesis 28:10-17).
- God was with Joseph when he was wrongly imprisoned in Egypt (Genesis 39:19-23).
- God promised to be with Moses when he addressed Pharaoh (Exodus 3:11-12).
- God met with God's people in the Tabernacle (Exodus 40:34-35).
- God stood with Joshua as he entered the Promised Land (Joshua 1:1-9).

- God told Gideon "I'll be with you" in his fight against the Midianites (Judges 6:11-16).
- The Spirit of God was with David from the moment he was anointed king (1 Samuel 16:13).
- God promised to be with Jeroboam even as the kingdom built by David was dividing (1 Kings 11:37-39).
- God was with Elijah in "a gentle and quiet whisper" on Mount Horeb (1 Kings 19:10-12).
- God is with us even in "the valley of the shadow of death" (Psalm 23:4, KJV).
- David acknowledged there was no escaping the presence of God (Psalm 139:7-12).
- God promised to be with the people of God and rescue them from exile (Isaiah 43:1-7).
- God promised to be with Jeremiah in his prophetic ministry (Jeremiah 1:7-8).
- Jesus promised to be with his disciples always (Matthew 28:18-20).
- God made known his presence to the Virgin Mary through an angelic announcement (Luke 1:26-28).
- God was with Paul in his many missionary excursions, doing miracles through him (Acts 19:11-12).
- The church became the new temple of God, where God would live and walk among creation (2 Corinthians 6:14-18).
- In the end, heaven and earth will reunite, and God will dwell forever with God's people (Revelation 21:2-5).

We reach the high point of this story of God-With-Us when we see Jesus, the Word of God, taking on human flesh and blood and moving into our neighborhood. This mysterious moment is when we saw "truth sprout[ing] green from the ground" (Psalm 85:11) and the unseen God became seen. The mystery of the incarnation was the culmination of all the moments in the biblical story when we saw God's presence with God's people. In Jesus, God has revealed the neighboring presence of God—because God desires to be a regular part of our everyday living and working and playing.

Before we turn our attention to our Scripture passage for this lesson, reflect on the following questions.

1. What kind of neighborhood did you grow up in as a child? Who were your neighbors? Did you feel safe? Does it still feel like home in your memory?

2. Can you recall a time in your life when you were very aware of the presence of God? Was this experience during a time of celebration? A time of crisis? Some other time?

3. If God showed up in your neighborhood today, what do you think that would look like? What might change?

The Word

John's Gospel, the fourth of four Gospel accounts in the New Testament, is different from the other three in its chronology of events and theological emphasis. John opens his Gospel not with the birth of Jesus in his humanity but with the glory of Jesus in his divinity—the Word who was with ("present to") God and the Word who *was* God (John 1:1). Calling Jesus the "Word of God" may seem a bit strange until you understand the background. The term translated "Word" is *logos*, which is a rich, complex Greek term. For the Greek philosopher Heraclitus, *logos* controlled the process of change in the natural world. *Logos* described the ordering principle that "guides everything through everything" and "relates all things to all things."[1] John made the bold proclamation that Jesus is that guiding principle, the *Logos*, that Greek-minded people of the first century believed had existed ever present among the gods and humanity.

The Word was first,
    the Word present to God,
    God present to the Word.
The Word was God,
    in readiness for God from day one.

JOHN 1:1-2

John doesn't open with the name Jesus but with the philosophically rich title *The Word*—a daring yet inviting way to begin his announcement about King Jesus. The Word, the ordering principle of the universe, predates all things and is preeminent over all things. *The Message* translation expands what is typically rendered as "the Word was with God" so we see that the Word was *present to* God. It takes the preposition *with* in this context as directional, denoting the Word's movement toward God. Thus the translation here: "the Word present to God, / God present to the Word." And then we read the shocking revelation—the Word *was* God!

Everything was created through him;
    nothing—not one thing!—
    came into being without him.
What came into existence was Life,
    and the Life was Light to live by.
The Life-Light blazed out of the darkness;
    the darkness couldn't put it out.

JOHN 1:3-5

The Word, known to the Greeks as a principle, is in fact the one true, living God who not only orders the universe but also created all things. In Greek philosophy, the Word was the uncreated controller of the process of change. John revealed that Jesus is the Word, the uncreated Creator. Everything else came into existence by the Word and through the Word. Notice the emphasis: "Not one thing!" came into being on its own. Life as we know it is neither self-evident nor self-producing but is itself a created gift given to us by the Word. And the gift of life is a light that the darkness of human despair cannot extinguish.

> There once was a man, his name John, sent by God to point out the way to the Life-Light. He came to show everyone where to look, who to believe in. John was not himself the Light; he was there to show the way to the Light.
>
> JOHN 1:6-8

Now John the Gospel writer gives us a human name: John, referring to John the Baptizer. This shifts our attention from the glories of heaven to the groundedness of history. The Word doesn't just exist in an unseen world but would soon be seen in the world of dirt and trees, people and places. John the Baptizer entered the story of Jesus as the forerunner, preparing the way for the Lord. John the Baptizer came to direct us to the Life-Light, which is not only the gift given to us by the Word but also is the Word of God himself. The Word is the very nature of God—life, light, and love.

> The Life-Light was the real thing:
> Every person entering Life
> he brings into Light.
> He was in the world,
> the world was there through him,
> and yet the world didn't even notice.
> He came to his own people,
> but they didn't want him.
> But whoever did want him,
> who believed he was who he claimed
> and would do what he said,
> He made to be their true selves,
> their child-of-God selves.

These are the God-begotten,
    not blood-begotten,
    not flesh-begotten,
    not sex-begotten.
JOHN 1:9-13

John testifies to the reality of Jesus as the Life-Light, the Word of God, rejected by the world and by his own people. But for those who wanted him, they were enabled to become their "true selves." All human beings are created in the image and likeness of God. We are all, in that sense, children of God. This is our principal identity. Nevertheless, when we believe in Jesus, we truly become who we were created to be. We are born anew by God and become children of God by faith.

The Word became flesh and blood,
    and moved into the neighborhood.
We saw the glory with our own eyes,
    the one-of-a-kind glory,
    like Father, like Son,
Generous inside and out,
    true from start to finish.
JOHN 1:14

The *Logos*, the guiding principle of the universe, which was life and light himself—present to God and one with God—took on flesh and blood. God saw us in our miserable state and chose not to stand far off and aloof but instead come to us in order to rescue us. The Word "moved into [our] neighborhood" to save the neighborhood. Early church father Athanasius writes, "It is we who were the cause of His taking human form, and for our salvation that in His great love He was both born and manifested in a human body."[2] The Greek word translated "moved into the neighborhood" (*skēnoō*) is a word that refers to setting up camp or dwelling, like God did in the Tabernacle. This might sound like a temporary move, but when God moved into the neighborhood, God came to take up permanent residence.

Take a moment to reflect on the following questions, based on this passage from the Gospel of John.

4. Why would John refer to Jesus as the *logos*, the Word, instead of using Jesus' given name?

5. Jesus was simultaneously *God* and *with God*. What does this seemingly paradoxical statement reveal about the nature of God?

6. What does the creation of all things by and through God communicate to us about God's greatness?

7. What images come to mind when you reflect on the words *life* and *light*? How do these images shape how you see Jesus at work in our world?

8. Has there been a period of time in your life when you've felt lonely? What was that experience like? How does it feel to know that God has moved into *your* neighborhood and is the ever-present God with you?

The Neighborhood

We find the seed for the theme of this Bible study, God in the neighborhood, in this one verse—John 1:14. And yet God's desire to dwell in and among God's people is a predominant theme throughout the story of Scripture. Jesus—God—moved into the neighborhood of block parties and backyard cookouts and cul-de-sac garage sales. Now Jesus makes his presence known in your neighborhood through you, through your love and acts of kindness. Jesus is the embodiment of kindness, which is mercy in motion. And Jesus has moved into your neighborhood to bring life and light.

9. What are some of the ways you see God at work in your neighborhood?

10. What is a specific act of kindness you can carry out in your neighborhood to demonstrate God's mercy?

The Prayer

As you come to the end of this lesson, the very heart of this Bible study series, turn your attention to the presence of God with you right now, in this very moment, and respond to God with this prayer.

Ever-present God of life and light, we acknowledge your presence with us. Thank you for moving into our neighborhood to rescue us. May your Kingdom come more and more among us as you are at work in our neighborhoods. Comfort the lonely. Heal the broken. Save the sinner. Grant that your people may have great awareness of your presence. In Jesus' name, amen.

LESSON 8

UNFORCED RHYTHMS OF GRACE

The Approach

I'm not the most coordinated person.

I'm six foot two and wear a men's size-14 shoe. I've been wearing at least size-13 shoes since I was thirteen years old. As a teenager, I loved sports, but I wasn't very good at any of the sports I tried—baseball, basketball, football, or dodgeball at school or tennis with my friends on warm summer evenings. I could always run fast, so that made up for some of my lack of athleticism, but I lacked hand-eye coordination, and my large feet, lanky arms, and skinny legs never seemed to move together in harmony. In high school, I ended up excelling at track, running 110-meter hurdles. After years of practice and training under the guidance of an all-state hurdling coach, I mastered the technique of gliding over the hurdles. (You don't jump hurdles, as I came to understand; gliding over them became an extension of my stride.) I found an outlet for my competitive nature in running hurdles.

Running in a straight line was one thing I found I could do; moving my body to a beat was another! I never attended any of my school dances. Self-consciousness and anxiety kept me at home. I had no interest in embarrassing myself on the dance floor at my high school. Things changed for me when I went off to college.

My college roommate invited me to go with him to a school dance during freshman-orientation week, so—reluctantly and begrudgingly—I went. Perhaps it was being in a new environment where hardly anyone knew me, or perhaps it was the restart many teenagers feel when they go off to college; whatever it was, I found myself on the dance floor on a random Thursday night at Truman State University in Kirksville, Missouri. The strangest thing happened to me that night: I cut my debilitating self-consciousness loose, stopped overthinking about what to do, and, for the first time, *felt* the music. Surprisingly, my feet began to move, almost on their own, to the beat of the music. My roommate said it was as if God had given me the spiritual gift of rhythm.

Later in life, I have begun to recognize a bad habit of retreating from the deep well of emotions in my soul and living too much in my head. I'm an analytical thinker, rational and deliberate about what I do and how I do it. Freeform dancing, on the other hand, isn't rational—*it's rhythmic.* It's not a matter of thinking through each step and trying to keep count of the beat (*1-2-3-4, 1-2-3-4*); rather, dancing requires us to surrender to the rhythm. While my dancing days ended with my freshman year of college, the lesson I learned that night stayed with me. Thinking clearly, and ultimately, Christianly, has its place in how we live our lives, but rationality isn't everything. God has created rhythms of grace for us to dance our way through ordinary, and at times extraordinary, days of our lives.

The single greatest mystery of the Christian faith is the incarnation, the Word taking on flesh and blood and moving into the neighborhood. God has joined us *as us* in order to rescue us.

The infinite took on the finite.

Immortality took on mortality.

The eternal took on the earthly.

God is here. God's neighboring presence is among us and for us to remake us. Our initial response to God's nearness is a kind of awakening. Before we can believe in the God who is present, we need to become *aware* of God's presence. Acceptance follows awareness. Once we acknowledge God's presence, we then respond to Jesus' invitation to come by faith into God's grand salvation story.

In this lesson we will wrestle with and reflect on what may be Eugene Peterson's most well-known line from *The Message*: "Walk with me and work with me—watch how I do it. Learn the unforced rhythms of grace" (Matthew 11:29). *The unforced rhythms of grace.* What a beautiful line. I wonder how many sermons have been preached using that as a title? How many books have been written that feature those words? Jesus invites us to approach him as the God-of-heaven-come-to-earth. Jesus welcomes us to learn to walk in rhythm with him, not overthinking on our own or stumbling in the dark but living—without force or manipulation—in the flow of God's grace.

Before we jump into Matthew 11 with more depth, reflect on the following questions.

1. Did you attend school dances as a teenager? Why or why not? If you did, what were they like for you?

2. Are you aware of God's presence with you? What are some ways you experience God's presence?

3. What are some of the ways you overthink things or "stumble around in the dark" (1 John 1:6) when faced with a decision—either monumental or commonplace?

The Word

Jesus had already called and commissioned his twelve apostles to go and proclaim the gospel, heal the sick, and drive out demons. He'd warned them: "Stay alert. This is hazardous work I'm assigning you. You're going to be like sheep running through a wolf pack, so don't call attention to yourselves. Be as shrewd as a snake, inoffensive as a dove" (Matthew 10:16). Jesus had sent word to John the Baptizer, who had asked if Jesus was "the One we've been expecting" (Matthew 11:3), that he had indeed been doing what the Hebrew prophets had said the Messiah would do. Jesus pronounced doom upon cities who had seen Jesus' miracles and yet failed to repent of their sins. Then Jesus, with a crowd surrounding him, broke into prayer:

> "Thank you, Father, Lord of heaven and earth. You've concealed your ways from sophisticates and know-it-alls, but spelled them out clearly to ordinary people. Yes, Father, that's the way you like to work."
>
> MATTHEW 11:25-26

God has moved into all our neighborhoods through Jesus and by the Spirit. God has moved into wealthy, gated neighborhoods, where the social elites and privileged live. God has also moved into ordinary neighborhoods filled with ordinary people who struggle with homelessness and food insecurity. Both groups of people have the opportunity to respond, but more often than not, it's the ordinary people who seem to see the truth of the gospel more clearly. The gospel sounds like good news to the ears of the marginalized, people experiencing poverty, the average, workaday folks. Conversely, the gospel often sounds like a challenge to the socially advantaged and the rich—after all, when you can provide for yourself everything you think you need, why would you need a Savior? So these folks often respond with disinterest and apathy.

> Jesus resumed talking to the people, but now tenderly. "The Father has given me all these things to do and say. This is a unique Father-Son operation, coming out of Father and Son intimacies and knowledge. No one knows the Son the way the

> Father does, nor the Father the way the Son does. But I'm not keeping it to myself; I'm ready to go over it line by line with anyone willing to listen."
>
> MATTHEW 11:27

Jesus sounds austere when speaking of unrepentant cities, but his tone changes when talking directly to the crowd in front of him. He appeals to those listening to understand his words of both challenge and comfort that come from his relationship with God the Father. Jesus makes the bold claim that "no one knows . . . the Father the way the Son does"—not the religious scholars, not the teachers in the synagogues, not even Moses and the prophets. Jesus, as the one and only Son of God, holds exclusive rights to the knowledge of God and God's saving plan for the world. Then Jesus extends an astonishing invitation:

> "Are you tired? Worn out? Burned out on religion? Come to me. Get away with me and you'll recover your life. I'll show you how to take a real rest."
>
> MATTHEW 11:28

Jesus spells out this invitation not for the self-contented souls happily living on the top of their empires of dirt, their lives built on the shifting sands of money and possessions, but for those who are tired, weary, and burned out. Religion has the potential to bring out the best in us, but sadly, both in Jesus' day and in ours, toxic and legalistic forms of religion can wear people out. The good news is that God has moved into our neighborhood. Jesus has come to us, promising life and rest, and now he invites us to come to him:

> "Walk with me and work with me—watch how I do it. Learn the unforced rhythms of grace. I won't lay anything heavy or ill-fitting on you. Keep company with me and you'll learn to live freely and lightly."
>
> MATTHEW 11:29-30

In most English translations, Jesus says something like "Take my yoke upon you" here (Matthew 11:29, NLT), an allusion to cattle being yoked together to pull a heavy load. To be yoked to Jesus means walking side by side with him and working alongside him in our neighborhoods. Unlike the yokes of moral duty, ethical codes, or religious legalism, Jesus' yoke is not burdensome. It allows us to "learn the unforced rhythms of grace" by which God created and sustains the world. We don't learn these rhythms by studying in a classroom; we feel the rhythms of grace in our souls more than we comprehend them in our minds. We cannot manipulate grace. Rather, we step into the flow of God's grace, where we find our true freedom.

Take a moment to reflect on the following questions.

4. Why didn't God come to the social elites of the first century so they could use their platforms of privilege to proclaim the Kingdom of God? Why come among shepherds, peasants, and fishermen instead of the powerful and materially wealthy?

5. Have you gone through a season of life where you've felt completely worn out? What did you do (or if you're in such a season now, what might you try) to restore your energy?

6. Have you ever felt burned out by religion? If so, what exactly burned you out, and how did you find life again? If not, have you known someone who has experienced religious burnout?

7. When you read the phrase *the unforced rhythms of grace*, what images come to mind? How do you feel when you reflect on this phrase?

8. What would it look like for you to "live freely and lightly" alongside Jesus?

The Neighborhood

If God has moved into our neighborhood, joining the human family as a human being, then God's presence can be found in *your* neighborhood. God is among us, but God's presence can be obscured from human view. People who are not aware of God's presence are living in our neighborhoods. The rapid pace of our busy, stressful, digitally infused world tramples down the God receptors of our hearts, creating an imperceivable disconnect between God and the people God loves. As we walk and work with Jesus, we have the opportunity, by our words and actions, to remind people that they are loved. In doing so, we can help them establish an unhindered connection to the God of grace. We don't need to force the gospel message on people. Rather, we can step into the rhythms of grace and see where the beat of God's love leads us.

9. Where have you seen signs of the presence of God in your neighbors?

10. What can you do to intentionally live in the unforced rhythms of grace among your neighbors?

The Prayer

As you conclude this final lesson on the incarnation, the wonderful mystery of God joining us in this embodied life of ours, offer this prayer.

> *Heavenly Father, you have made all things. You are the Creator and Sustainer of all things great and small, seen and unseen, remembered and forgotten. Thank you for your presence among us, in our neighborhood, and in our lives. Give us eyes to see you at work in our neighborhood. Give us hearts that are responsive to the nudging of the Holy Spirit, prompting us to remain in the flow of the unforced rhythms of grace. All this for your name's sake, amen.*

AS WE GO

We've completed our walk through eight studies of Scripture. The beauty of *The Message* translation has helped us uncover some details in the Scriptures that can spark a fresh imagination to see what God has promised and what God has accomplished by sending his one and only Son. Our reflection on the mystery of the incarnation—God taking on flesh and blood—is not just a *helpful* practice for Advent and Christmas; it's a *hopeful* practice for our entire lives as followers of Jesus.

The central hope of the gospel is the truth that we are not alone. God meets us in and through Jesus and promises to be with us "day after day after day, right up to the end of the age" (Matthew 28:20). In a world marked by isolation and injustice, God moved into the neighborhood, offering the comfort of a neighbor and setting right a world gone wrong. As we reflect on God's neighboring presence with us, we awaken to the work of God around us. We become aware that we do, in fact, live in a God-saturated world.

God has joined us; that's what God has done. We awaken to God's presence; that's what we do. Since God is with us, though we may experience doubt and worry, we won't be overcome by them. God is at work—even though at times that work is imperceptible. Our God is working, which is "why we can be so sure that every detail in our lives of love for God is worked into something good" (Romans 8:28). As our hearts are renewed in this hope, we can live as a peaceful people bringing hope and life in our neighborhoods.

ACKNOWLEDGMENTS

I am a believer in the power of the Holy Spirit to work with Holy Scripture when the holy people of God study and discuss Scripture together. To that end, I have been writing Bible study discussion questions for the local church for decades. I have added reflection questions to all the books I have written. For years I have written discussion questions for groups to wrestle with together alongside the content of the sermons at my local church. I've been humbled by the kind responses from individuals and groups of people who have found my questions thought-provoking and helpful. The God in the Neighborhood Bible Studies are my first attempt at a comprehensive, multivolume Bible study written for the local church for individual and group use. I'm grateful for the support and encouragement of so many who have made these Bible studies possible.

I'm grateful for the team at NavPress. As a high school student, I participated in The 2:7 Series discipleship course published by NavPress, and now, some thirty years later, I'm thrilled to be able to write a Bible study series to add to the NavPress catalog of discipleship resources. I appreciate the enthusiasm of David Zimmerman and Olivia Eldredge for this project. Since the first day I pitched the idea for a Bible study using the beauty and particularity of *The Message*, you have both given me unwavering support. Olivia, it has been a joy to work with you in the editorial process. You have a strong sense for how readers engage with the Scriptures and with my writing and reflection questions. Your keen insights and constant encouragement have made my writing better. Yay! Thanks to Elizabeth Schroll for your careful editorial work. It has been a true pleasure to work with you on this project.

Thank you also to the number of people who gave me feedback on titling and content for these studies. I'm grateful to Joe Beach, who shares a love for Eugene Peterson and *The Message*, for his suggestions and input. Thanks to fellow author and Bible study enthusiast Kat Armstrong for reading my first lesson and providing me with helpful feedback. Thanks also to the members of Word of Life Church in St. Joseph, Missouri, who attended many of the Bible studies I led during Advent 2023 and Eastertide 2024. Your discussions during those Bible studies gave shape to this series.

An unmistakable thank you is due to my wife, Jenni, who remains my faithful confidant and supporter. Thank you for giving up many Fridays when I was tucked away writing these Bible studies. Thanks to my sons, Wesley, Taylor, and Dylan. One book in this series is dedicated to each of you with a blessing. Each of you, in your own way, makes me so proud! Thank you to Maggie and my grandsons, Leo and Sam, for rounding out the Vreeland clan. I love you all so much. Thanks to my brother, Jeff, and my father, Ed, for all your support and for cheering me along as I write.

Finally, I'm deeply grateful for the impact Eugene Peterson has had on my life as a pastor, author, lover of Scripture, and follower of Jesus. My family gave me a copy of *The Message Devotional Bible* for Father's Day some time ago. While I had regularly referenced *The Message* over the years, I hadn't taken the time to read it daily until 2023 and 2024. I looked forward to my Bible reading during that season because *The Message Devotional Bible* not only provided me with Peterson's helpful contemporary translation but also offered notes from him along the way. I treasured spending those mornings with Eugene and his beautiful translation. These Bible studies, using *The Message*, are a way for me to extend my gratitude and to help, in a small way, to keep the life and legacy of Eugene Peterson alive. I love you, Eugene. Thanks for showing me the way.

NOTES

AS WE BEGIN | AN INTRODUCTION TO INCARNATION

1. Eugene H. Peterson, "A Sort of Homecoming," *The Message Devotional Bible: Featuring Notes and Reflections from Eugene H. Peterson* (NavPress, 2018), 1069.
2. "Language and the way we use it in the Christian community are the focus of this conversation on the spirituality of language. Language, all of it—every vowel, every consonant—is a gift of God. . . . I want to tear down the fences that we have erected between language that deals with God and language that deals with the people around us. It is, after all, the same language." Eugene H. Peterson, *Tell It Slant: A Conversation on the Language of Jesus in His Stories and Prayers* (Eerdmans, 2008), 2, 4.

LESSON 1 | GOD RULES

1. Matthew W. Bates, *Why the Gospel? Living the Good News of King Jesus with Purpose* (Eerdmans, 2023), 27.

LESSON 2 | PLAYING WAR NO MORE

1. G. K. Chesterton, *Orthodoxy*, reprint (Image Books, 2001), 45. First published in 1908 by Dodd, Mead & Co.
2. Eugene H. Peterson, "Isaiah," *The Message Devotional Bible: Featuring Notes and Reflections from Eugene H. Peterson* (NavPress, 2018), 761.
3. Walter Brueggemann, *The Prophetic Imagination*, 2nd ed. (Fortress Press), 2001.
4. Kat Armstrong, *Mountains: Rediscovering Your Vision and Restoring Your Hope in God's Presence* (NavPress, 2023), 2.

LESSON 4 | A VIRGIN WILL GET PREGNANT

1. Irenaeus, *Against Heresies* III.22.4, in *Ante-Nicene Fathers, Volume 1, The Apostolic Fathers, Justin Martyr, Irenaeus* (Hendrickson, 1994), 455.
2. Irenaeus, *Against Heresies* III.22.4, 455.

LESSON 6 | MESSIAH AND MASTER

1. Rich Villodas, "Keeping Christ in Christians," Missio Alliance, December 8, 2016, https://www.missioalliance.org/keeping-Christ-Christians.

LESSON 7 | THE WORD IN THE NEIGHBORHOOD

1. Eva Brann, *The Logos of Heraclitus: The First Philosopher of the West on Its Most Interesting Term* (Paul Dry Books, 2011), 21.
2. St. Athanasius, *On the Incarnation* 1.4. See https://www.ccel.org/ccel/athanasius/incarnation.ii.html.

Also by Derek Vreeland

ECPA Book Award Finalist

In *Centering Jesus*, Derek Vreeland invites us to imagine what it looks like to keep Jesus, the Lamb of God, at the center of three key areas of our lives—our spiritual formation, our moral lives, and our common life together. With the deep divide in American culture and the polarization that continues to grow, we need a renewed focus on the Lamb so that we might blaze a path forward into civility and kindness.

Learn how to

- identify the problems that occur when Jesus is obscured from our view
- walk through key biblical descriptions of the Lamb
- describe a Lamb-shaped and Jesus-centered approach to the Christian virtues of faith, hope, and love, the foundation of our moral lives
- experience the Lamb at the center of common life together—specifically, worship life, participation in acts of justice, and political life

Available at NavPress.com and wherever books are sold.

Published in alliance with Tyndale House Publishers

CP2084